The Love of God Is a Root of Evil

Glenn Bell, Ph.D.

© 2020 Glenn B. Bell

All rights reserved. This book or any portion thereof may not be reproduced or used in any manner whatsoever without the express written permission of the publisher except for the use of brief quotations in a book review or scholarly journal.

First Printing: 2020

ISBN 978-1-7328379-3-5

Front Cover Photo

Depiction of human sacrifice to Molech

By Charles Foster - Illustrators of the 1897 Bible Pictures and What They Teach Us http://associate.com/photos/Bible-Pictures--1897-W-A-Foster/page-0074-1.jpg, Public Domain, https://commons.wikimedia.org/w/index.php?curid=11785813

Note: Use of this photo as well as all other figures in the book does not in any way suggest endorsement of this book.

The Love of God Is a Root of Evil

Table of Contents

Preface 9

Introduction 11

Part 1 – Origin, Purpose, and Validity of Religion 13

Chapter 1 Origin of Religions 13

    Earliest Religions 15

    Canaanite Religion 18

    Greek and Roman Religions 19

    Hinduism 21

    Zoroastrianism 24

    Jainism 25

    Taoism 27

    Buddhism 28

    Shintoism 32

    Christianity 33

    Islam 36

    Sikhism 38

    Mormonism 39

    Rastafarianism 41

    Wicca 42

    Raëlism 43

Discussion 44

Chapter 2 – Key Questions Addressed by Religion 47

Where did we come from? 47

Judeo/Christian/Islamic 48

Greek Mythology 52

Sumerian Mythology 54

American Indian Mythology 56

Buddhism 59

Zoroastrianism 62

Hinduism 63

Discussion 65

What is the purpose of life? 66

Judaism 66

Christianity 67

Hinduism 67

Buddhism 68

Islam 69

Shintoism 70

Wicca 70

Discussion 70

What Happens after Death? 72

Christianity 73

    Islam 74

    Hinduism 75

    Buddhism 77

    Discussion 78

Chapter 3 Purpose of Religions 83

    Getting What You Want During Life 83

    Societal Control 88

    Religion as a Social Club 93

    Religion as a Business 94

    Discussion 97

Chapter 4 Validity of Religions 99

    Group 1 – Judaism, Christianity, and Islam 99

        Judaism 99

        Christianity 100

        Islam 100

    Group 2 – Hinduism, Buddhism, Jainism, and Sikhism 109

        Hinduism 109

        Buddhism 110

        Jainism 110

        Sikhism 111

    Group 3 – Ancient Greece, Rome, and Egypt 113

        Ancient Greek Religion 113

Ancient Roman Religion 114

Ancient Egyptian Religion 114

Discussion 115

Part 2 Implications of Religion 119

Chapter 1 Community 119

Discussion 122

Chapter 2 Acceptable and Unacceptable Behaviors 123

Ethics in Buddhism 124

Ethics in Hinduism 125

Sin in Islam 126

Sin in Judaism 127

Dress Codes 132

Gender Inequality 134

Slavery 135

Dietary 137

Medical Care 139

Discussion 140

Chapter 3 Positive Aspects of Religion 141

Promotion of Moral Behavior 141

Good Deeds 142

Discussion 144

Chapter 4 Persecution 145

Inquisition 150

Witch Trials 152

Sikh Protests 154

ISIS 155

Discussion 156

Chapter 5 Religious Wars 157

Jewish Warfare (2000 BCE-present) 157

Muslim Conquests (624-present) 158

Sunnis Against Shias (632-present) 159

Crusades (~1096-1272) 161

Muslim Piracy Against Christians (1492-1587) 164

Muslims Against Christians (1520-1530) 164

Abyssinia – Somalia (1529-1559) 166

Second War of Kappel (1531) 167

French Wars of Religion (1562-1598) 170

Eighty Years' War (1568-1648) 171

Thirty Year's War (1618-1648) 172

Barbary Wars (1801-1815) 172

Muslim Jihad Against Allied Powers in WWI (1914) 173

Pakistan and India (1947-present) 174

Buddhist Uprising in Vietnam (1954-1966) 175

First Sudanese Civil War (1955-1972) 176

Lebanese Civil War (1975-1985) 177

Second Sudanese War (1983-2005) 178

Yugoslav Wars (1991-1995) 178

Nigerian Conflict (1999-2015) 179

9/11 Attack on the Twin Towers (2001) 180

Discussion 181

Conclusion 183

Acknowledgements 187

Index 189

About the author: 192

Endnotes 193

Preface

Thank you for considering reading this book. I entitled the book "The Love of God Is a Root of Evil" as a parody to the verse 1 Timothy 6:10, which reads as "For the love of money is the root of all evil: which while some coveted after, they have erred from the faith, and pierced themselves through with many sorrows" in the King James Version.

While I will not argue that coveting after money can lead to evils, there are many sources of evil. You might think that loving God would be a good thing and some good actions could come from such a motivating factor. What I examine is this book is what affect religion has on the behavior of human beings. I am generally equating religion and the love of God (or gods). I hope that you will agree with me that the counterintuitive finding is that religion can be and has shown itself as a root of evil.

Some might readily agree that love of a false god (or gods) would lead to evil but love of the true God (or gods) would not lead to evil. There is considerable debate as to who is right and wrong about religion. So, I also look at the credibility of some religions. I do not attempt to discuss all religions as there are too many and it would detract from the point of the book. Suffice it that I tried to cover the most popular religions.

If when you are done with the book you disagree with the points made, then that is fine. I hope that you have gained some thoughts to consider. If you found it insightful, then that is even better.

Note: This is a second version of this book, which is an attempt to improve the clarity and organization. In the previous version I used the pen name Vorbi Wahrheit to avoid potentially harmful repercussions but since the book went unnoticed, I have changed the strategy.

Introduction

In part one of this book I will discuss the origins and purpose of religion as well as the validity or lack of validity of various religions. The origins of many religions are well known in history, but the origin of some ancient religions is less understood. The purpose of religions is more speculative but hopefully my speculations are sufficiently backed by evidence and logic that you will be able to agree with these points.

To evaluate the credibility of religions I will investigate the claims of various religions and the evidence in support of such claims. I will use different types of information to examine these claims, including literature, science, history, and logic. I will sometimes state that a certain claim of a religion is not consistent with science. You might say "well then, science is wrong." While you are welcome to that opinion, I believe the problem with such a claim is that although there is sometimes refinement of science, science is based on observations and facts. Much of religion is based on faith in doctrines that are without evidence or are claimed to not need evidence. I believe that the reliability of science and logic is greater than that of faith. Some may say that science and logic address different areas of thought than does religion and faith, but I think that science and logic have implications on the claims of religion. Thus, when a religious teaching is inconsistent with science and logic, I will recommend that science is more likely correct than the disparate claim of the religion.

In part two of this book I will discuss the impact of religion on individuals, societies, and humanity. I will examine how religious beliefs impact an individual's behavior and how people treat others with and without the same religious beliefs. I will also examine the psychology of the treatment of those of similar and dissimilar religious beliefs and whether religion has a positive or negative effect on society. Much of the discussion related to societal impact will be based on historical information but we will also look at religion's impact on our current society. I think you will find it difficult to disregard the acts of abuse and violence, and the wars that are conducted in the name of religion and as an act of love to one's God (or gods).

Part 1 – Origin, Purpose, and Validity of Religion

Chapter 1 Origin of Religions

I begin by defining what I mean when using the term religion. One definition of religion is "belief in and worship of a supernatural controlling power (as in God or gods)"[i]. Usually it is the case that a religion has belief in a God or gods but some religious belief systems may not include a god such as in Jainism, where godliness is a quality of every soul. Jainism will be discussed in more detail later. Another definition is that a religion is "a collection of cultural systems, beliefs, and world views that establishes symbols that relate humanity to spirituality and, sometimes to moral values"[ii]. This is closer to the definition that I will use in this book. It is interesting to note that there is no legal definition of a religion for tax purposes in the United States. Instead, tax exemptions are allowed for churches, not religions. 'To be a "church" a religious organization must engage in the administration of sacerdotal [relating to priests or the priesthood] functions and the conduct of religious worship in accordance with the tenets and practices of a particular religious body[iii].' Religion is a term that is often applied to forms of organized worship of a God or gods but I will use the term loosely to also include other ritualistic belief systems.

It is estimated that over 4,000 religions have existed worldwide[iv] many of which currently have some adherents. Most of the world's population is affiliated with one of the following religions: Christianity, Islam, Hinduism, Confucianism, Taoism, and Buddhism[v]. Of course, the population of the Earth changes and the popularity of various religions changes over time. Below is some information on the number of adherents for various religions from 2005.

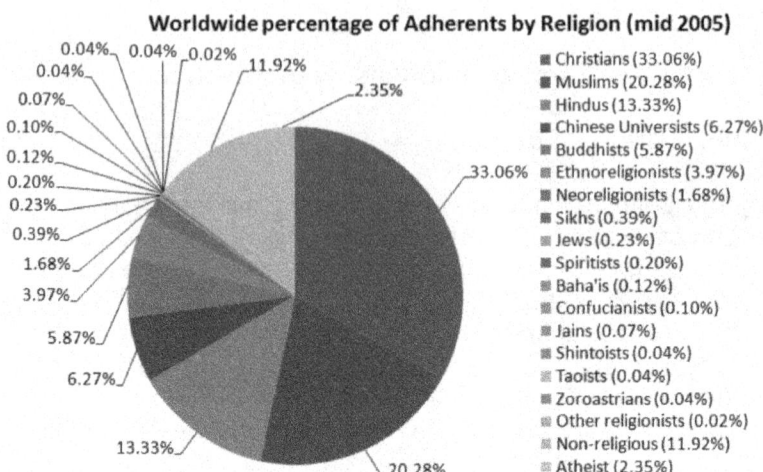

Worldwide Percentage of Adherents by Religion (mid 2005)[vi]

In this book, I will discuss the claims and practices of the more populous religions, although I will touch on some other religions as well. Some of the religions I will discuss were more popular in the past and have historical value. Although we will discuss religions with certain labels such as Christianity or Judaism, religions evolve over time[vii] and when I refer to a specific religion it is likely that the current version of the religion is different from the original version of the religion. This is especially the case with modern versions of ancient religions.

Religions originate in specific geographical areas but tend to spread to groups of people in other localities. Typically, the spread is to adjacent territory, but it is not always the case. For example, Islam started in Mecca, Saudi Arabia but it has spread to many areas of the world. Several of the most popular religions originated in the middle east (Judaism, Christianity, and Islam) and another group of important religions originated in India/Pakistan (Hinduism, Buddhism, Jainism, and Sikhism), but religions have origins that vary over many geographical locations. The location of origin of the religion is usually the place where the founder lived. Below is a map showing geographically where some religions have the most adherents using data from 2011.

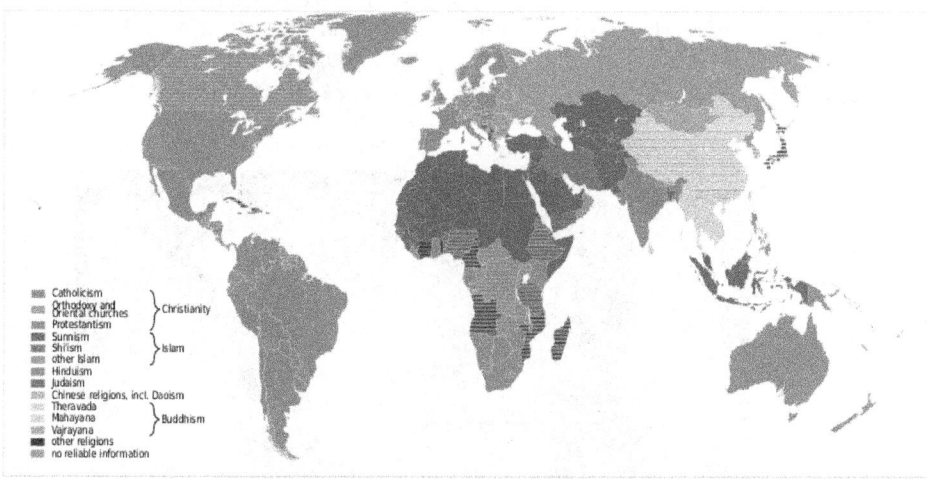

World map coded to denote major religion affiliations (as of 2011)[viii]

People of the same religion often identify with others of the same religion and have a kinship based on their religion. Some religions have geographically diverse adherents. Some adherents' beliefs many vary within the same locality but are more likely to deviate from one another in disparate locations. If there is disagreement in beliefs or doctrines, this may lead to the development of sects within a religion. These disagreements in beliefs can lead to varying levels of dispute. These disagreements can lead to an attempt to cleanse the religion of heresy, which will be discussed later in this book.

Origins

In the sections below I will provide a historical discussion of the origins of some popular religions.

Earliest Religions

It is difficult to know when the first religions originated or whether religious beliefs were present in other animals, for example other hominoids, which may predate humans. Some possible evidence of early religions can be pointed to by Venus figurines, which appeared in graves during the Paleolithic Period mostly in Europe as early as 35,000 BCE[ix]. Such a religion may have been matriarchal, which focused on a goddess or goddesses.

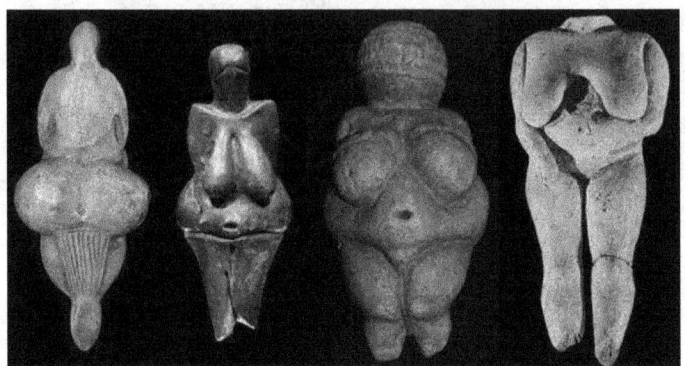

The Venus Figurines of the European Paleolithic Era[x]

There is archeological evidence of burial rituals (including putting red ochre on the corpses) and various items being placed in graves as early as 19,000 BCE[xi]. This may be evidence of belief in an afterlife, which is a common theme in many religions. Many early religions were polytheistic and included forms of sacrifice or offerings to the gods in an attempt to obtain favorable treatment by the gods. Such religions include the Proto-Indo-Europeans (4000-1000 BCE)[xii]. Most of these Indo-European religions included belief in deities, religious practices, and a belief in the afterlife.

The Pyramid Texts from ancient Egypt, which are carved on the walls and sarcophagi, are some of the oldest known religious texts dating from around 2350 BCE[xiii].

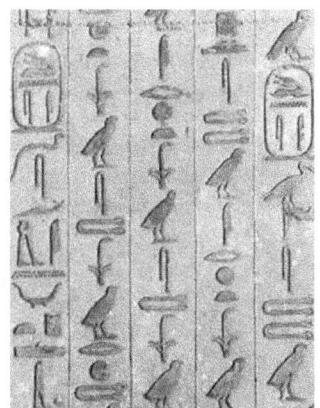

The Pyramid Texts are a collection of ancient Egyptian religious texts[xiv]

Stonehenge was completed around 2300 BCE[xv] and it may to have had some religious significance based on human bones found at the site and its potential use as a solar calendar. The Minoan Civilization in Crete worshipped a variety of goddesses (2200 BCE)[xvi]. Hindu beliefs were recorded in the Rig Veda (1700-1100 BCE). The Hindu Bhagavad Gita, written later, revealed that many gods were subject to a supreme Brahman god[xvii]. The religions of many ancient cultures were polytheistic, including Assyria, Babylonia, Egypt, Greece and Rome. These belief systems viewed gods as being in control of all natural events such as rainfall, harvests and fertility. Pantheism (a belief that all is god) prevailed in numerous ancient cultures. The belief that the Universe itself was divine was typified in the animism beliefs of the African and American Indian cultures, the later Egyptian religion under the Pharaohs, and Buddhism, Confucianism and Taoism in the cultures of the Far East.

The earliest monotheistic religion was Judaism although there was some evidence of a monotheistic period in Egypt under Akhenaten. The Zoroastrians (6000 BCE) believe in Ahura Mazda, who is the supreme God above all but this is not strictly monotheistic[xviii].

The following is a graphic that provides an approximate timeline for the origin of a variety of religions. I suspect there may be some potential disagreement on a few of the dates on the graph but the exacts are not critical to the book.

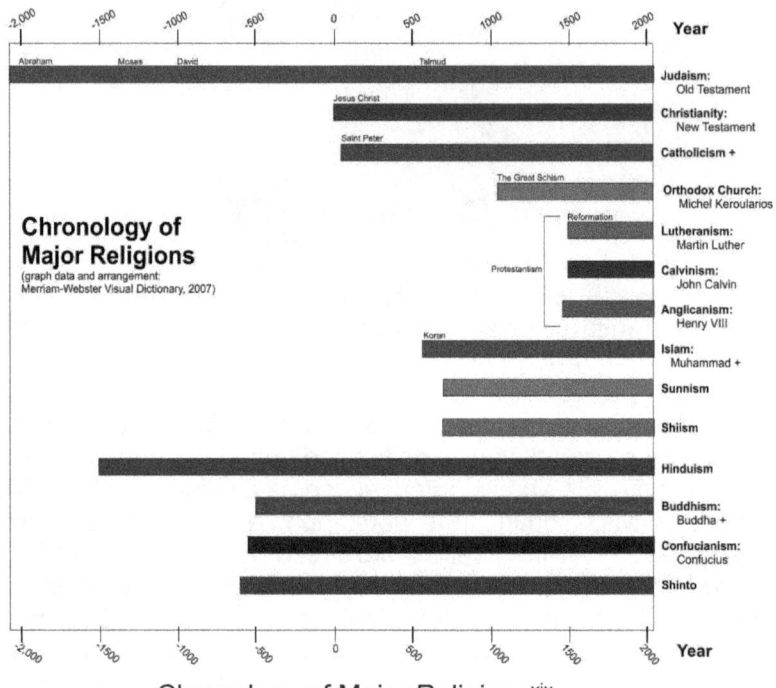

Chronology of Major Religions[xix]

We have determined that although we do not know when the first religion was invented or originated, we know that religions have ancient origin. Let us look at some specific religions for which we have some historical knowledge.

Canaanite Religion

Ancient Semitic religions (third millennium BCE) practiced by the Canaanites included sacrifice to the male god, Baal, and his female counterpart, Ashtoreth, among other gods[xx].

Ashtoreth[xxi]

Baal controlled the rain and the harvest, while Ashtoreth controlled fertility and reproduction. Canaanites believed that following physical death, the soul departed from the body to the land of death[xxii]. "Bodies were buried with grave goods, and offerings of food and drink were made to the dead to ensure that they would not trouble the living. Dead relatives were venerated and sometimes asked for help.[xxiii]"

Greek and Roman Religions

The Greeks and Romans developed a structured pantheon of gods and goddesses. In Greek theology (developed out the Proto-Indo-European religion), there was a hierarchy of deities, with Zeus, the king of the gods, having a level of control over all the others, although he was not almighty. Some deities had dominion over certain aspects of nature. For instance, Zeus was the sky-god, Poseidon ruled over the sea and earthquakes, Hades ruled over the realms of death and the Underworld, and Helios controlled the Sun[xxiv]. Rome added to this collection of gods to include both Greek gods as well as a number of gods of foreign cults. Roman religion includes the major gods: Jupiter (god of justice, law, sky, and thunder), Neptune (god of the sea), Pluto (god of the underworld) and Juno (god of family and marriage) as well as a number of "minor" gods and goddesses including

Nemesis, the god of revenge; Cupid, the god of love; Pax, the god of peace; and the Furies, goddesses of vengeance.

Judaism

Judaism arose in the eastern Mediterranean in the second millennium BCE. Judaism has its origins in the polytheistic Semitic religions including the Canaanite religion[xxv]. During the ninth century BCE, the Israelite religion became distinct from other Canaanite religions due to its monotheistic worship of Yahweh. This religion is based on the writings of the Old Testament. One of the main tenants of Judaism is that God created a chosen race from the lineage of Abraham to be the Jews. Judaism was originally localized to the lands of Israel incorporating the northern and southern tribes. The religion focuses on temple worship including animal sacrifice at the temple in Jerusalem. After the destruction of the first (Solomon's temple) and the second (Herod's temple) temples, Judaism was modified and it no longer practices many of the teachings outlined in the Torah including commandments pertaining to the temple including animal sacrifice.

Model of Jerusalem, Herod's Temple[xxvi]

This new version of Judaism, rabbinic Judaism, is what is currently practiced. Rabbinic Judaism is centered around the teachings and writings of Rabbis[xxvii]. Prayers were added to replace the sacrificial offerings and synagogues have become the central places of worship instead of the temple. Rabbis in some sense replaced priests. This evolution of Judaism poses some problems, since the promises of Yahweh regarding the land of Israel and the prosperity of the Israelites appear to not have been fulfilled and Yaweh's temple has been destroyed (see below)[xxviii]. Admittedly, the temple could be rebuilt in the future but there has been and likely will continue to be generations of Jews that are unable to practice temple worship as described in the Torah.

Genesis 13: 14-18

> The Lord said to Abram after Lot had parted from him, "Look around from where you are, to the north and south, to the east and west. All the land that you see I will give to you and your offspring **forever**. I will make your **offspring like the dust of the earth, so that if anyone could count the dust, then your offspring could be counted**. Go, walk through the length and breadth of the land, for I am giving it to you." So, Abram went to live near the great trees of Mamre at Hebron, where he pitched his tents. There he built an altar to the Lord.

Exodus 25: 8-9

> Let them **make a sanctuary for me so I may live among them**. This is how you are to make it: according to all that I'm showing you, according to the pattern for the tent and the pattern for all its furnishings."

Hinduism

Hinduism developed from the religion that the Aryans (Indo-Iranians) brought to India with them in around 1900-1400 BCE[xxix]. Although Hinduism contains a broad range of philosophies, it is linked by shared concepts, recognizable rituals, cosmology, shared textual resources, and pilgrimage to sacred sites. Hindu texts include the Vedas and Upanishads considered to be eternal knowledge authored by neither a human or a divine agent. Other texts include the Sutras and Shastras, which are written by human authors. Prominent themes in Hindu beliefs include the four aims of human life[xxx]:

- Kama (pleasures and passions)
- Artha (prosperity or success)
- Dharma (duty or virtue)
- Moksha (release, freedom, and salvation)

Hindu practices include rituals such as worship, recitations, meditation, family-oriented rites of passage, annual festivals, and occasional pilgrimages. Some Hindus leave their social world and material possessions and engage in lifelong monastic practices. Hinduism prescribes duties, such as honesty, refraining from injuring living beings, patience, forbearance, self-restraint, and compassion. Hinduism includes a diversity of ideas on spirituality and traditions, has no ecclesiastical order, no unquestionable religious authorities, no governing body, no prophets, or any binding holy book. Hindus can choose to be polytheistic, pantheistic, monotheistic, monistic, agnostic, atheistic, or humanistic.

There are two major schools of Hinduism: Vedanta and Yoga[xxxi]. In Vedanta, one is to discover the truth of oneself and the Universe, by being alive to what is in all areas of one's life. One is to live intelligently and fully, freeing one from sorrow, fear, and all forms of limitations. Yoga includes following ethical values and attitudes, prayers, doing postures and breathing techniques, concentration of the mind, and meditation practices. The goal of Yoga is an absorption of the mind, which culminates in liberation.

Hinduism can be subdivided into a few major currents. The four major modern currents of Hinduism are associated with their primary deity or deities: Vaishnavism (Vishnu), Shaivism (Shiva), Shaktism (Devi), and Smartism (five deities treated as same). Hinduism also accepts numerous divine beings, with many Hindus considering the deities to be aspects or manifestations of a single impersonal absolute or ultimate reality or God, while some Hindus maintain that a specific deity represents the supreme and various deities are lower manifestations of this supreme. Below are a few of the many Hindu deities[xxxii].

Vishnu[xxxiii]

Durga[xxxiv]

Ganesha[xxxv]

Other notable characteristics of Hinduism include a belief in the existence of the soul, reincarnation, and karma [sum of a person's actions relevant to deciding fate in the future] as well as a belief in dharma [principle of cosmic order]. Hindus believe that all living creatures have a soul. The soul is believed to be eternal. Most

Hindus observe religious rituals at home. The rituals vary among regions, villages, and individuals. Devout Hindus perform rituals such as worshiping at dawn after bathing (usually at a family shrine, and typically includes lighting a lamp and offering food before the images of deities), recitation from religious scriptures, singing devotional hymns, yoga, meditation, and chanting mantras.

Zoroastrianism

Zoroastrianism has its origin in Yazd, Iran. It is ascribed to the Iranian prophet and philosopher Zoroaster. Zoroastrianism exalts Ahura Mazda as its supreme being. Major features of Zoroastrianism, including Messianism, heaven and hell, and free will, have influenced other religious systems, including Judaism, Gnosticism, Christianity, and Islam.

19th century Indian-Zoroastrian perception of Zoroaster derived from a figure that appears in a 4th century sculpture at Taq-e Bostan in south-western Iran[xxxvi]

Zoroastrianism has recorded history in the 5th-century BCE. It served as the state religion of the Iranian empires from around 600 BCE to 650 CE. Zoroastrianism was suppressed from the seventh century onwards following the Muslim conquest of Persia of 633–654. Current estimates place the number of Zoroastrians at around 190,000, with most of them living in India and in Iran[xxxvii]. In Zoroastrianism, the purpose of life is to "be among those who renew the world...to make the world progress towards perfection." Its general concepts include:

- Good Thoughts, Good Words, Good Deeds
- There is only one path and that is the path of truth
- Do the right thing because it is the right thing to do, and then all beneficial rewards will come to you

Zoroastrian theology includes a duty to protect nature. In Zoroastrianism, water and fire are agents of ritual purity, and the associated purification ceremonies are considered the basis of ritual life. Fire is considered a medium through which spiritual insight and wisdom is gained, and water is considered the source of that wisdom. Zoroastrians believe that Ahura Mazda will ultimately prevail over the evil, at which point the Universe will undergo a cosmic renovation and time will end. In the end, all of creation will be reunited in Ahura Mazda, returning to life in the undead form. A savior-figure will bring about a final renovation of the world in which the dead will be revived.

Depiction of Ahura Mazda[xxxviii]

Jainism

Jainism is a nontheistic religion founded in India that teaches the way to liberation and happiness is to live lives of harmlessness and renunciation[xxxix]. Jainism was established by Mahavira around 500 BCE[xl]. Jainism is like Buddhism in that both developed as a dissension to the Brahmanic philosophy that was dominant during the period in north-east India.

Statue of Mahavira[xli]

Jainism and Buddhism share a belief in reincarnation, which leads to liberation[xlii]. The essence of Jainism is a concern for the welfare of all beings and for the health of the Universe. Jains take the following five vows:

- non-violence
- truth
- no stealing
- chastity
- non-attachment

Ascetic life may include nakedness symbolizing non-possession of even clothes, fasting, body mortification, penance, and other austerities. Asceticism helps to burn away past karma and stop producing new karma, both of which are believed to be necessary for reaching liberation from rebirths and for salvation. Jains believe that animals and plants, as well as humans, have souls. Each soul is considered of equal value and should be treated with respect and compassion.

A male human is considered to have the closest potential to achieve liberation, particularly through asceticism. There are two major sects in Jainism: Digambaras and Svetambaras, which have different views on ascetic practices. Digambaras believe women must gain karmic merit to be reborn as a man and then they can achieve spiritual liberation. Svetambaras believe that women are capable of the same spiritual accomplishments as men[xliii].

Taoism

Taoism or Daoism is a religious or philosophical tradition of Chinese origin, which emphasizes living in harmony with Tao (The Way)[xliv]. Taoist ethics emphasize effortless action, naturalness, simplicity, spontaneity, and the three treasures (compassion, frugality, and humility). Taoism originated in China around 2000 years ago. Early Taoism is based on notions from the School of Yin-yang (opposite or complementary forces), and is influenced by the Yijing (Book of Changes). The Yijing proposes a philosophical system about how to keep human behavior in accordance with the cycles of nature. Over time Taoism has evolved. Hundreds of variations in Taoist practice exist. There are two main schools within Taoism: "philosophical Taoism" and "religious Taoism." Philosophical Taoism focuses on the philosophical writings of Lao-Tzu, Chuang-Tzu, and other mystics. Religious Taoism emphasizes religious rituals aimed at attaining immortality[xlv]. The current day rituals in Taoism are elaborate and must be conducted perfectly[xlvi]. Festivals are presided over by a Grand Master who officiates these celebrations.

Statue at Mount Qingyuan of Lao-Tzu, Chinese philosopher who lived around 500 BCE and founded Taosim[xlvii]

Taoism includes many deities, that are worshipped in Taoist temples[xlviii]. The deities include the Jade Emperor (great high God, rules Heaven), First Principal (has no beginning or end, self-existing, limitless, invisible), Three Pure Ones (different manifestations of Lao Tzu), Three Officials (ruler of Heaven, ruler of Earth, ruler of Water), Three Epochs (ruler over winter and spring, ruler over summer, and ruler over fall), and Eight Immortals (deities modeled on historical figures who live in Heaven).

Taoism promotes[xlix]:

- achieving harmony or union with nature
- the pursuit of spiritual immortality
- being virtuous
- self-development

Taoist practices include:

- meditation
- feng shui – a Chinese metaphysical and quasi-philosophical system that seeks to harmonize individuals with their surrounding environment[l]
- fortune telling
- reading and chanting of scriptures

Buddhism

Buddhism originated in India between the sixth and fourth century BCE. It is a religion attributed to the teachings of Siddhartha Gautama (Buddha). It is believed that Buddha was born in Nepal and was moved by the suffering of humanity. Buddha studied under Vedic teachers learning meditation and ancient philosophies, including the concept of "nothingness, emptiness" and "what is neither seen nor unseen." Finding these teachings to be insufficient, he turned to the practice of asceticism. He also found asceticism insufficient and he turned to the practice of meditation. He gained insight into the workings of karma and about moderation as the path to end suffering from rebirths. He attracted followers and founded a monastic order.

A statue of Buddha from Sarnath, Uttar Pradesh, India, 4th century CE[li]

Buddhists number around 488 million worldwide[lii], making it one of the world's major religions.

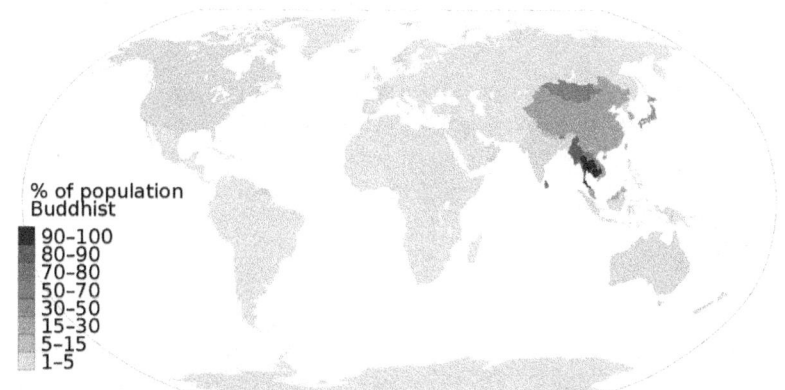

Buddhism percent population in each nation[liii]

There are two major branches of Buddhism: Theravada and Mahayana. Practices of Buddhism include taking refuge in the Buddha, the Dharma [cosmic law and order], and the Sangha [community]. It also involves the study of scriptures, observance of moral precepts, renunciation of cravings and attachment, the practice of meditation, and the cultivation of wisdom, loving-kindness, and compassion.

In Theravada Buddhism, the ultimate goal is the cessation of the five obstacles (ignorance, egoism, attachment, aversion, and clinging to life) and the attainment of Nirvana, achieved by practicing the Noble Eightfold Path. This is believed to enable the escape from the cycle of suffering and rebirth. The Noble Eightfold Path[liv] includes:

1) right view
2) right resolve
3) right speech
4) right conduct
5) right livelihood
6) right effort
7) right mindfulness
8) right meditative absorption or union

This is considered only possible for monks or nuns. Laity can only hope to be reborn into monastic life.

In Mahayana Buddhism a path is available to all people as opposed to only monks or ascetics. They believe that enlightenment can be attained in a single lifetime. It includes veneration of celestial beings, Buddhas, religious rituals, and use of icons.

Confucianism

Confucianism was developed from the teachings of the Chinese philosopher Confucius (551-479 BCE), who promoted the concept of a ritualized life[lv].

Portrait of Confucius[lvi]

Confucius was inspired by the statesman Zhougong (eleventh century BCE, Zhou dynasty), who was said to have helped consolidate, expand, and refine the feudal ritual system. The feudal system was based on blood ties, marriage alliances, and covenants as well as on newly negotiated contracts[lvii]. The appeal to cultural values and social norms for the maintenance of order was based on ethical and religious power by the mandate of heaven and social solidarity is to be achieved by ritual observance.

Confucianism focuses on the cultivation of virtue and maintenance of ethics[lviii]. The five virtues of Confucius are:

- Ren, benevolence, charity, and humanity
- Yi, honesty and uprightness
- Xin, faithfulness and integrity
- Li, correct behavior or propriety
- Zhi, knowledge

Confucianism holds people in contempt for failure to uphold the moral values of Ren and Yi. Confucianism is a source of the values and social code of the Chinese. Its influence has extended to other countries, particularly Korea, Japan, and Vietnam.

Shintoism

Shintoism is the ethnic religion of Japan that focuses on ritual practices to establish a connection between present-day Japan and its ancient past[lix]. Shinto practices were first recorded in the eighth century. The earliest Japanese writings do not refer to a unified "Shinto religion," but instead to a collection of native beliefs and mythology. Shintoism has no canonical scriptures or authoritative set of beliefs[lx]. Shintoism is based on a belief in and worship of kami. Kami is the sacred power in both animate and inanimate objects. Kami are not gods. They are spirits that are concerned with humans[lxi]. From the sixth century, onwards it was accepted that the Emperor was descended from the kami, was in contact with them, and was often inspired by them[lxii].

Shintoism is not concerned with instructing people on how to live. Shintoism focuses on discovering ways of communicating with kami. The kami can respond to prayers, can influence natural forces, and human events. The focus of Shintoism is on the ritual of offering to the kami and communicating with it. Izanami and Izanagi are the two most famous kami because they are seen as the creators of the Earth[lxiii]. They are also the parents of multiple kami, who rule over the moon, Sun, fire, water, Earth, and netherworld. Izanami is a female kami whereas Izanagi is a male kami. Izanami is the passive (yin) essence and Izanagi is the active (yang) essence. The two balance each other out.

Izanagi and Izanami - Kobayashi Eitaku[lxiv]

Shinto shrines can be in the home and there are also public shrines. Shinto festivals include purification and offerings.

Oomatono Tsunoten Shinto Shrine in Inagi, Japan[lxv]

Christianity

Christianity came into being in the Roman occupied city of Jerusalem during the first century CE. Christianity originated from within Judaism. The religion is centered around the teachings of Jesus Christ. The basis of the religion is acceptance of Jesus

Christ as the Son of God. The meaning of Jesus being the Son of God has been debated. Most of Christianity claims that Jesus is God. A common belief of Christianity is that Jesus was born of the virgin Mary. Jesus was crucified by the Romans. Christians believe that shortly after his death, Jesus was resurrected from the dead and went to heaven.

Pietro Perugino's depiction of the Crucifixion as Stabat Mater, 1482[lxvi]

Another key belief in Christianity is the trinity. Although the term is not used in the Bible, God is described as having three parts: God the father, God the Son (Jesus), and God the Holy Spirit (or sometimes referred to as the Holy Ghost). Some claim that this belief makes Christianity polytheistic, but this is generally not felt to be the case.

Christianity claims the writings of Judaism (including the Torah) as part of their religion. Christianity did not see significant growth until after the conversion of Constantine, approximately 312 CE. Constantine stopped Christian persecutions and legalized Christianity in the Roman Empire in the Edict of Milan in 313.

Marble head representing Emperor Constantine[lxvii]

There are several major branches of Christianity: Catholic (which believe that the Pope is the head of the church), Eastern Orthodox (which do not believe that the Pope is the head of the church), Oriental Orthodox (are separated from Catholic and Eastern Orthodox over differences in Christology)[lxviii], and Protestantism (started by Martin Luther in response to concerns with the Catholic church including indulgences).

While I mentioned a few key differences, there are other differences in beliefs among these groups in Christianity. Protestantism includes many denominations including Lutheran (originated in 16th century, associated with Martin Luther), Presbyterian (originated in 16th century, associated with John Calvin), Baptist (originated in 17th century, John Smyth founded first Baptist church in Amsterdam)[lxix] and Methodist (originated in 18th century, associated with the teachings of John Wesley). These denominations disagree with each other in some doctrines and/or practices.

Islam

Islam originated in the seventh century CE. In 610 CE, Mohammed claimed to obtain special revelation from God (Allah) through the archangel Gabriel, which was written down in a book called the Quran.

Muhammad receiving his first revelation from the angel Gabriel. From the manuscript Jami' al-tawarikh, 1307[lxx]

The Quran is considered the unaltered and final revelation of God. Islam is the world's second largest religion and fastest growing religion in the world[lxxi]. Religious concepts and practices include the Five Pillars of Islam and following Islamic law. The Five Pillars of Islam are:

1) the creed, "I testify that there is no god but God, Muhammad is the messenger of God."
2) daily prayers
3) almsgiving
4) fasting during Ramadan
5) pilgrimage to Mecca

This monotheistic religion is closely related to Christianity and Judaism. Muhammad's message was accepted by some who became followers and was met with opposition from some in Mecca, where Muhammad was born and lived for most of his first 52 years. After persecution of the Muslims, Muhammed and his followers moved to Medina. After a series of battles with Arab tribes, Muhammed united the tribes of Arabia under Islam.

After Muhammad's death in 632, disagreement broke out over who would succeed him as leader of the Muslim community. The dispute intensified after the Battle of Karbala[lxxii], in which Muhammad's grandson Hussein ibn Ali was killed. The issue of succession divided the early Islamic community and led to division of Islam into sects. Most Muslims are of one of two sects: Shia (believing that Ali and his descendants should rule) or Sunni (accepting others as rulers).

Sunnis are a majority in most Muslim communities in Southeast Asia, China, South Asia, Africa, most of the Arab World. Sunni Islam has four schools of jurisprudence including the Hanafi, Maliki, Shafi'i, and Hanbali. Shias are about 25 to 30 percent of the entire Muslim world. They also have several different schools of thought. Another school of Islam is called Ibadism (developed out the Islamic sect Khawarji around 650 CE).[lxxiii]

The main Islamic schools of law of Muslim countries or distributions[lxxiv]

The expansion of the Muslim Empire in the years following the Prophet Muhammad's death led to the creation of the caliphates [areas ruled by Muslim leaders], occupying various areas. Conversion to Islam was increased by missionary activities of Imams, who intermingled with the people to propagate the religious teachings[lxxv]. Muslim dynasties and empires were established such as the Abbasids (caliphs of Baghdad), Fatimids in North Africa and Egypt, Almoravids in Morocco, Seljukinds in West and Central Asia, Ajuran, Adal, and Warsangali in Somalia, Mughals in India, Safavids in Persia, and Ottomans in Anatolia.

Sikhism

Sikhism is a religion founded in India in the late 15th century. Its members are known as Sikhs[lxxvi]. According to Sikh tradition, Sikhism was established by Guru Nanak[lxxvii] (1469–1539) and subsequently led by a succession of other Gurus.

Fresco of Guru Nanak[lxxviii]

The fundamental beliefs of Sikhism are written in the sacred scripture Guru Granth Sahib[lxxix]. Some main principles of Sikhism include[lxxx]:

- Belief in one God
- Salvation through meditation on God
- All human races and sexes are equal
- Simple vegetarian diet
- Hair is not to be cut
- No belief in superstitions
- Selflessness
- Promotion of wellbeing of all
- Universal peace and prosperity

- Liberty, equality, and fraternity
- Universal brotherhood
- Immortality of the soul
- Actions and deeds affect karma

Two Sikh gurus: Guru Arjan[lxxxi] (1563 –1606) and Guru Tegh Bahadur[lxxxii] (1621 –1675), after they refused to convert to Islam were executed by the Mughal rulers. Persecution of Sikhs prompted the founding of the Khalsa[lxxxiii], as a warrior order to protect the freedom of religion. The Khalsa tradition was initiated in 1699 by Guru Gobind Singh after the beheading of his father Guru Tegh Bahadur.

In Sikhism, one should control or eliminate the five vices of ego, anger, greed, emotional attachment, and lust, known as the Five Thieves[lxxxiv]. People vulnerable to the Five Thieves are separated from God and are not fulfilling the purpose of their lives. Sikhs believe in reincarnation and karma concepts found in Hinduism and Buddhism. There are Sikh sects that believe in an alternate lineage of Gurus, or have a different interpretation of the Sikh scriptures, or believe in following a living guru, or other concepts that differ from the orthodox Khalsa Sikhs.

Mormonism

Mormonism[lxxxv], also known as the Church of Jesus Christ of Latter-day Saints, is a Christian sect that was founded by Joseph Smith in Western New York in the 1820s. Mormonism was taught by Smith in the 1840s. After he was killed in 1844, most Mormons followed Brigham Young on a westward journey to the area that became the Utah Territory. Brigham Young[lxxxvi] supervised the journey of 60,000 to 70,000 pioneers to the Salt Lake Valley in Utah from Illinois and other staging points. Mormons believe in the Bible, as well as other books of scripture, such as the Book of Mormon.

Portrait of Joseph Smith[lxxxvii]

The Book of Mormon[lxxxviii] is a sacred text of the Latter-day Saints, which has discussions on the fall of Adam and Eve, the nature of the atonement, eschatology, redemption from physical and spiritual death, and the organization of the latter-day church. A key event in the book is an appearance of Jesus Christ in the Americas after his resurrection.

Their beliefs include that God the Father, Jesus Christ, and the Holy Ghost (the Godhead) are three separate beings, who are in one purpose. The Father and Jesus Christ have physical bodies. After death, the soul goes to a spirit world, where they receive instruction and are later reunited with their bodies[lxxxix]. Good Mormons live forever in Heaven with God and their families, good non-Mormons are rewarded but do not have the presence of God, and those who reject the Godhead even after instruction go to Hell.

Some Mormons have openly practiced polygamy. Mormons dedicate significant time and resources to serving in their church, and many Mormons choose to serve as missionaries. According to Mormons, every person will be resurrected, and nearly all of them will be received into various kingdoms of glory. To be accepted into the highest kingdom, a person must fully accept Christ through faith, repent, and partake in ordinances such as baptism and the laying on of hands.

Rastafarianism

Rastafarianism, is an Abrahamic religion [belief in Abraham as a prophet]. It is considered as a religious movement and a social movement. It developed in Jamaica during the 1930s and has heterogeneity among practitioners. Rastafari theology[xc] was developed from the ideas of Marcus Garvey (1887-1940), a political activist who wanted to improve the status of blacks.

Marcus Garvey – Civil Rights Activist[xci]

Rastafarians believe that blacks are the chosen people of God. Through colonization and slave trade their role has been suppressed.

Rastafarians believe in a single God, Jah, who partially resides within each individual. Rastafarians believe reincarnation follows death and that life is eternal. The former emperor of Ethiopia, Haile Selassie, is a central figure in the religion. Many Rastas regard him as an incarnation of Jah on Earth and as the Second Coming of Christ. Others regard him as a prophet.

Emperor Haile Selassie I of Ethiopia[xcii]

Rastafari focuses on the displaced African population, which it believes are oppressed by Western society. Many Rastas seek the resettlement of the African population in either Ethiopia or Africa, referring to this continent as the Promised Land of Zion. Others seek the adoption of an Afrocentric attitude while living outside of Africa. Communal meetings are typically include music, chanting, discussions, and the smoking of cannabis.

Wicca

Wicca is a contemporary Pagan religious movement (others include Druidism and Heathenism). It was developed in England during the first half of the 20th century and was introduced to the public in 1954 by Gerald Gardner[xciii]. Wicca is typically duotheistic, worshipping a Goddess and a God. These Gods are often viewed as the Mother Goddess[xciv] and the Horned God, respectively.

These deities may be regarded in a henotheistic [worshipping one god while not denying the existence of other deities] way. For this reason, they are sometimes referred to as the "Great Goddess" and the "Great Horned God", with "great" meaning a deity that contains many other deities within its own nature. These two deities are sometimes viewed as facets of a greater pantheistic divinity, which is regarded as an impersonal force or process rather than a personal deity. Wiccan beliefs can range from polytheism to pantheism, even to Goddess monotheism. Although different Wiccans attribute different traits to the Horned God, he is most often associated with animals and the natural world, but also with the afterlife. He is viewed as an ideal role model for men. The Mother Goddess has been associated with life, fertility, and the springtime, and is an ideal role model for women. Gerald Gardner promoted the belief in reincarnation, which is accepted by many Wiccans. Many Wiccans believe in magic as a force exercised through the practice of witchcraft or sorcery. The majority of Wiccans follow a code known as the Wiccan Rede, which states "an it harm none, do what ye will."

Raëlism

Raëlism is a Unidentified Flying Object religion that was founded in 1974 by Claude Vorihon, French former automobile journalist and race car driver. He claims to have had alien encounter with beings who gave him knowledge of the origins of all major religions. For over 30 years, Claude Vorilhon, Raël, has been the leader of this movement[xcv].

Claude Vorrilhon[xcvi]

This movement teaches that life on Earth was created by humanoid extraterrestrial, which are called Elohim[xcvii]. Raëlians do not believe in a god (or other deity), but in extraterrestrials. Raëlians believe that members of the Elohim civilization sent different prophets, including Moses, Jesus, Buddha, and others to guide humanity and to prepare humans for the future, which were created as a result of a sexual union between a human woman and one of the Elohim.

They do not believe in a soul that exists free of the physical world. Raëlians believe that computers of the Elohim are recording the memories and DNA of humans. People will be brought back from the dead and judgements will be made based on the actions of their past life.

Raëlans believe in[xcviii]:
- Self-love - accepting ourselves as we are
- Self-respect - this requires a healthy lifestyle that only be achieved by being in harmony with nature
- Accountability - all humans are responsible for their actions
- Respect for life - do not kill human life
- Respect for others - accept our differences
- Sharing - every human has the right to food, a place to sleep, clothes, and an education
- Democracy
- Non-violence
- World peace - creation of a world government supported by peacekeepers
- Femininity - politeness and love

Raëlians founded Clonaid, a company that envisions that human beings will be scientifically recreated though a process of human cloning, and Clitoraid, an organization whose mission is to oppose female genital mutilation.

Discussion

Many religions have evolved from other religions through the influence of concepts derived from religious figures throughout history. Since religions are founded by disparate figures over geography and time, they are generally in disagreement with each other to varying degrees. As is the case with many ideas, existing ideas are generally modified with some innovation to generate alternative concepts. Religions appear to follow this general methodology. There appears to be at least two main streams of religious thought. The one branch of beliefs is a view, which has its origins in middle east, which includes Judaism, Christianity, and Islam. Each is built on the foundations of the other. These religions are considered monotheistic and are concerned with attaining eternal life in heaven or paradise. Additionally, these three faiths are religions of "the book," since they claim to have authority based on inspired scripture.

Another main branch is associated with Hinduism, Jainism, Buddhism, and Sikhism. The subsequent religions to Hinduism are largely reactions to Hinduism that are started by specific gurus. These religions often have a focus on how to live one's life and may incorporate belief in reincarnation principles.

Precursors and co-existent religions to these two branches of religion tend to be mythological and polytheistic. Often believers in one religion have tried to suppress other religions by various means including war. This will be discussed later.

One may ask which religion is correct, but a more important question is whether any of them are correct. We shall examine this issue in Chapter 4.

Thus, we have examined:

- How did the different religions originate?
- Why are there so many different religions?

Next, we will look at different aspects of why religions exist.

Chapter 2 – Key Questions Addressed by Religion

One purpose of religions is an attempt to provide answers to questions on the origin of mankind and the Universe, the purpose of life, and what happens after death. Although this is not an exhaustive list of important questions addressed by religion, these are some key questions. Religions often try to address these issues and to make claim to knowledge of truth related to these concerns. Let us examine the answers to these questions provided by some religions and examine what are reasonable answers based on alternate sources including science and logic. While some may claim that science, history, and logic are unable to answer some of these difficult questions, let us examine whether the answers provided by religion make sense based on facts and logic.

Where did we come from?

Common questions of most rational humans include "Where did we come from?" or "How did we get here?" More fundamental is the question of the origin of the Universe and not merely the origin of our own beings. Religions often tell us that a God or gods created the Universe (all that exists). This begs the question of where the God or gods came from. The usual answer is that God did not come from anywhere. God (or gods) is eternal, always existing, and God is beyond our comprehension. While this is not an intellectually satisfying answer, it is not impossible depending on one's definition of God. It is worth noting that although scientific explanations for the origin of the Universe provide significant explanations, ultimately the scientific explanation leads to an equally unsatisfying answer about the origin of all matter and/or energy. Alternatively, some pantheistic religions claim everything composes God (God and the Universe are equivalent).

When considering the origins of the Universe, life, and humans, I believe that it is worth considering the vastness of the Universe and the composition of living beings as well as our physical world. The Earth is one planet in a vast Universe that is composed of perhaps around 180 billion galaxies with on average 100 billion planets.

Living beings such as animals, plants, and bacteria are composed of cells (at least on Earth). These cells are composed of a combination of atoms, which are composed of sub-atomic particles such as electrons, protons, and neutrons. Albeit we can take this analysis further to elementary particles (such as quarks, leptons, bosons), let it suffice that all of the physical world (organic and non-organic) appears to be composed of the same building blocks, which may or may not include dark matter. Thus, all known matter (including all living beings) are made of atomic particles and there is no scientifically valid evidence of any additional component to living beings such as a soul or spirit, but we will discuss souls and spirits more completely later.

Let us look at the question of our origin from the perspective of some specific religions.

Judeo/Christian/Islamic

Judaism, Islam, and Christianity all claim that God created the heavens, Earth, and all living things in six days, per the book of Genesis in the Bible, albeit many interpret the scriptures as allegorical. A day may be a meaningless measure of time when the Earth and Sun are not in existence (a day being defined as the time the Earth completes one full rotation in reference to the Sun). Regardless of the time period involved, the book of Genesis[xcix], chapter 1, places the order of events as the following:

Day 1 God created the heavens and the Earth
The "heavens" is thought to refer to everything beyond the Earth, (i.e. outer space). The Earth is made but not formed in any specific way, although water is present. God then speaks light into existence. He then separates the light from the dark and names the light "day" and the dark "night." It is difficult to determine where the light comes from, since the Sun is not created until day 4 (see below).

Day 2 God creates the sky
The sky forms a barrier between the water upon the surface of the Earth and the moisture in the air. At this point the Earth would

have an atmosphere.

Day 3 God creates dry land
Continents and islands are above the water. The large bodies of water are named "seas" and the ground is named "land." God also creates all plant life.

Day 4 God creates all the stars and heavenly bodies
Two great heavenly bodies are made in relation to the Earth. The first is the Sun, which is the primary source of light and the moon, which reflects the light of the Sun. The movement of these bodies will distinguish day from night. This is a bit confusing considering day and night were introduced in day 1.

Day 5 God creates all life that lives in the water
Any life of any kind that lives in the water is made at this point. God also makes all the birds.

Day 6 God creates all the creatures that live on dry land. This includes every type of creature not included on previous days and man.

The Quran also states that God created the heavens and Earth in six days.

Surah 11:7
> And it is He who created the heavens and the earth in six days - and His Throne had been upon water - that He might test you as to which of you is best in deed. But if you say, "Indeed, you are resurrected after death," those who disbelieve will surely say, "This is not but obvious magic."

Among the many issues with this account, it makes little sense to have plant life on the Earth on day 3 and the Sun and stars on day 4, since plants require sunlight. Additionally, we have the Earth created on day 1 and all other planets and the Sun on day 4. This is not consistent with a scientific understanding of the origins of the Universe. We have a detailed knowledge of the beginning of the Universe, which has been scientifically studied, which includes the origin of our solar system through the big bang[c]. The age of the

Universe has been scientifically estimated to be around 13.8 billion years old[ci] based on studies of microwave background radiation, and measurements by the Planck satellite, and the Wilkinson Microwave Anisotropy Probe[cii], which is not consistent with the age of the Universe per Genesis. We have visual evidence of galaxies that are billions of light years away from the Earth from telescopes such as the Hubble Space Telescope[ciii]. If the Universe were much younger, God would have had to generate light in motion to the Earth from these distant galaxies.

Genesis describes man as created by God. Genesis 1:27 states,

> "So God created man in his own image, in the image of God he created him; male and female he created them."

Genesis 2:21-23 states:

> "So the Lord God caused the man to fall into a deep sleep; and while he was sleeping, he took one of the man's ribs and then closed up the place with flesh. Then the Lord God made a woman from the rib he had taken out of the man, and he brought her to the man. The man said, 'This is now bone of my bones and flesh of my flesh; she shall be called woman, for she was taken out of man.'"

Additionally, we see that the Genesis account has mankind originating from a special act of creation on a single day and later woman being made from the rib of man. The concept of creation in a single day, the concept of special creation, and the idea that woman was made from the rib of man are not consistent with our scientific understanding of the origin of mankind. It is not consistent with paleontological evidence. Evolution of man from other primates through gradual variation in genetic traits is well established[civ]. Fossils and genetic evidence support the evolutionary origin of mankind[cv]. Studies in genetics and molecular biology have explained the occurrence of the hereditary variations that are essential to natural selection. Genetic variations result from changes, or mutations, in the nucleotide sequence of DNA, the molecule that genes are made from. Such changes in DNA now can be detected and described with great precision[cvi]. Hundreds of thousands of fossils, found in well-dated rock sequences, represent successions of forms through time and manifest many evolutionary transitions. Microbial life of the simplest type was already in existence 3.5 billion years ago. The oldest evidence of more complex organisms (that is, eucaryotic cells, which are more complex than bacteria) has been discovered in fossils sealed in rocks approximately 2 billion years old. Below is a depiction of the evolution of some of the different species over time.

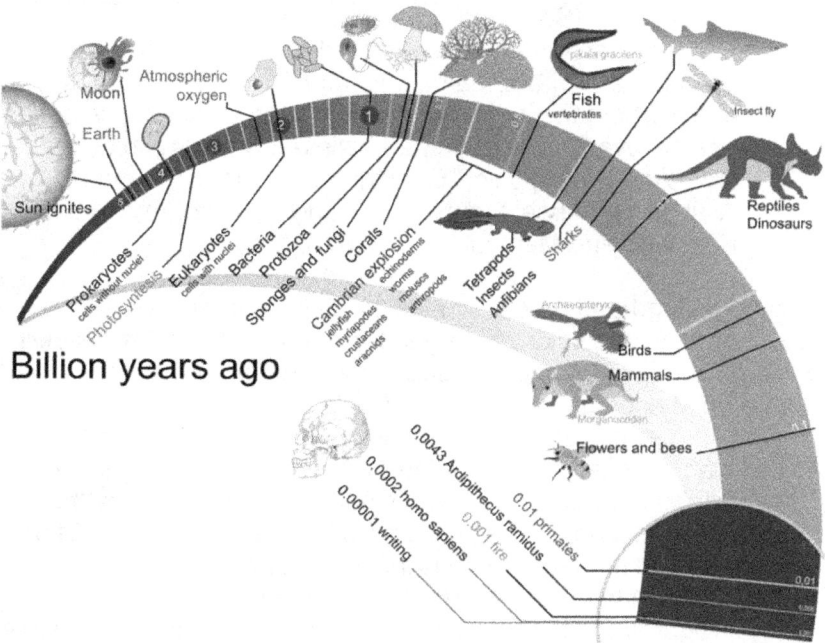

Timeline of Evolution of Life[cvii]

According to Genesis, subsequent to the spread of mankind from Adam and Eve a world-wide flood was believed to have occurred. This event was to have killed all air-breathing life except that which were saved in the ark. Noah was to have built a large boat (ark), which housed these animals during the period of the flood. This event is described in Genesis and in the Quran (also the Epic of Gilgamesh).

Quran 11:37-41:
> And construct the ship under Our observation and Our inspiration and do not address Me concerning those who have wronged; indeed, they are [to be] drowned." And he constructed the ship, and whenever an assembly of the eminent of his people passed by him, they ridiculed him. He said, "If you ridicule us, then we will ridicule you just as you ridicule. And you are going to know who will get a punishment that will disgrace him [on earth] and upon whom will descend an enduring punishment [in the Hereafter]." [So it was], until when Our command came and the oven overflowed, We said, "Load upon the ship of each [creature] two mates and your family, except those about whom the word has preceded, and [include] whoever has believed." But none had believed with him, except a few. And [Noah] said, "Embark therein; in the name of Allah is its course and its anchorage. Indeed, my Lord is Forgiving and Merciful."

This huge flood and rescue of land animals in an ark is inconsistent with a scientific understanding of the various species of life on Earth. This is discussed in more detail later (See Sumerian Mythology).

From science, it can be concluded that the Genesis account is at odds with the laws of nature. While some would like to say that the Genesis description is consistent with science; it is not. Thus, we may conclude that science is incorrect, or the author of Genesis was either incorrect or was writing in an allegorical manner regarding creation. Also, the story regarding the flood has a similar problem.

Greek Mythology

Hesiod, a Greek poet (8th century BC) provides an account of the creation myth in his poem Theogony[cviii]. The following is a synopsis of the early acts of the creation myth[cix]:

"In the very beginning, Chaos, the nothingness out of which the first objects of existence appeared, arose spontaneously. The parthenogenic [asexually reproduced] children of Chaos were Gaia (the Earth), Eros (Desire or sexual love), Tartarus (the Underworld), Erebus (Darkness) and Nyx (Night).

Erebus and Nyx reproduced to make Aither (Brightness) and Hemera (Day), and from Gaia came Ouranos (Sky), the Ourea (Mountains) and Pontus (Sea). Ouranos mated with Gaia to create three sets of offspring: the twelve Titans (Oceanos, Coeus, Crius, Hyperion, Iapetos, Theia, Rhea, Themis, Mnemosyne, Phoebe, Tethys and Kronos), a race of powerful deities that ruled during the legendary Golden Age; the three Cyclops (Brontes, Steropes and Arges), a race of one-eyed giants; and the three Hecatonchires (Kottos, Briareos and Gyges), hundred-handed giants of even greater power and ferocity than the Titans.

Ouranos was so disgusted with the Hecatonchires that he pushed them back into Gaia's womb, so Gaia begged the Titans to punish their father. Only Kronos, the youngest and most ambitious Titan, was willing to do so, and he castrated his father with Gaia's sickle. Ouranos' blood splattered onto the earth, producing the Erinyes (the vengeful Furies), the Gigantes (Giants) and the Meliai (a race of tree nymphs). Kronos threw Ouranos' severed testicles into the sea, and Aphrodite (the goddess of Love) formed out of the sea-foam which resulted.

Nyx produced many children, including Moros (Doom), Oneiroi (Dreams), Ker and the Keres (Destinies), Eris (Discord), Momos (Blame), Philotes (Love), Geras (Old Age), Thanatos (Death), the Moirai (Fates), Nemesis (Retribution), the Hesperides (Daughters of Night), Hypnos (Sleep), Oizys (Hardship) and Apate (Deceit). Eris, in her turn, produced Ponos (Pain), Hysmine (Battles), the Neikea (Quarrels), the Phonoi (Murders), Lethe (Oblivion), Makhai (Fight), Pseudologos (Lies), Amphilogia (Disputes), Limos (Famine), Androktasia (Manslaughters), Ate (Ruin), Dysnomia (Lawlessness), the Algea (Illnesses), Horkos (Oaths) and Logoi (Stories).

After Ouranos's castration, Gaia married Pontus and they went on to produce a line of sea deities, nymphs and monsters, including Nereus (the Old Man of the Sea, also known as Proteus and

Phorcys in his other aspects, from whom were descended the Nereids, the fifty nymphs of the sea, the best-known being Thetis), Thaumas (who later married the Oceanid Electra, and bore Iris, or Rainbow, and the two winged spirits, Aello and Ocypetes, known as the Harpies), Eurybia and Cetus (a hideous sea monster)."

This explanation of creation is counter to any scientific explanation (see scientific discussion of the origin of the Universe above). The process of giving human qualities such as emotions, motivation, and procreative acts to the physical world is easily seen as the creative capabilities of humans.

Sumerian Mythology

The Sumerians inhabited southern Mesopotamia, modern day Iraq, around 4500 BC. The main source of information about the Sumerian creation myth is in the prologue to the Epic of Gilgamesh, which describes the process of creation[cx].

Originally, there was only Nammu, the primeval sea. Then, Nammu gave birth to An, the sky, and Ki, the Earth. An and Ki mated with each other, causing Ki to give birth to Enlil, the god of wind, rain, and storm. Enlil separated An from Ki and carried off the Earth as his domain, while An carried off the sky. The complete list of gods includes several hundred.

Tablet V of the Epic of Gilgamesh. The Sulaymaniyah Museum, Iraq[cxi]

The gods, some of which were described earlier, created people and created the animals. A god was put to death, and his body and blood was mixed with clay. From that material, the first human being was created, in likeness to the gods. This first man was created in Eden. In the Epic of Gilgamesh, Eden is mentioned as the garden of the gods and is located somewhere in Mesopotamia between the Tigris and Euphrates rivers. Initially human beings were unable to reproduce but were later modified with the help of Enki [god of water] and Ninki [goddess of plants].

This story parallels in several ways the story of the creation of mankind in the book of Genesis (discussed earlier) and in the Quran. In Genesis the first man is also made of clay (Genesis 2:7) and in the Quran God created man from clay (Quran 23:12-15), which a consistent theme in other religions and mythologies. In Genesis 2:15 man is said to have been placed in Eden. The Quran also refers to Eden as the first abode of Adam and his wife.

These versions are equally inconsistent with our scientific understanding of the origin of mankind.

The Sumerian mythology continues with, the kingship descending from heaven to found the first cities. The gods decided not to save mankind from an impending flood. The king learns of this, warns a hero, and gives him instructions for making an ark. A huge storm rocks the boat for seven days and seven nights. Then the Sun god appears, and the king creates an opening in the boat, prostrates himself, and sacrifices oxen and sheep. Once the flood is over, the animals disembark and the king prostrates himself before the sky-god and the chief of the gods, who give him eternal life.

This flood story in the book of Gilgamesh is like that of the story of Noah in Genesis and in the Quran.

The flood in the Bible describes the demise of humans and animals, except those that inhabited the ark. While there is evidence of regional floods and it is possible that some people could have survived a large flood in an ark type of ship, it is not logical that such a flood would be world-wide nor would it be practical for all of animal life to be kept and survive in an ark (especially as described in the Bible). There is evidence that there was a large flood when the Euphrates and Tigris rivers overflowed but this was a localized flood[cxii].

The ark is too small to include all the different species of animals. The genetic diversity of life cannot be derived from the small number of animals that could be housed in the ark. The ethnic complexity of humans found throughout the world cannot be derived from the flood survivors in the few centuries since that time[cxiii]. It is unclear how one would supply the proper food types and quantity for all the animals during the flood. Additionally, there would be a significant problem with the generation of waste and ventilation. The variety of animals also have climatic requirements that could not be met leading to death of some types of animals. Note that fish are generally not tolerant of sudden changes in temperature, salinity, or pH of water. A massive flood would have significant impact on the rivers, ponds, seas, and oceans. Additionally, much of plant life would be destroyed by the saltwater. This would in turn lead to starvation for the animals that theoretically were released from the ark.

American Indian Mythology[cxiv]

Cherokee

According to Cherokee mythology, the Earth is a great island floating in a sea of water and suspended at each of the four cardinal points by a cord hanging down from the sky vault, which is of solid rock[cxv]. Originally, the animals exist, and they live in the sky. Land isn't formed until the water beetle explores what is at the bottom of the large body of water and comes back with mud, which then becomes the land. At first the Earth was flat, soft, and wet. Other animals wanted to come down to the new earth and birds were sent to see if the mud was dry. A large buzzard was sent to the Earth while it was soft. Where the buzzard's wings struck the Earth, a valley was formed and where they turned up a mountain was formed. After the mud dried, the Earth was dark, so the animals put the sun in a track to run east to west.

The animals and plants were made first. The first people were a brother and sister. The brother hit his sister with a fish and told her to multiply after which she gave birth every seven days. Once there were too many people women were forced to have a child once a year.

This account is not consistent with our scientific understanding of the origin of the Universe, Earth, and life. The origin of the creatures in the sky is not provided. There is no evidence of a large water beetle capable of bringing up mud to generate all the land area of the Earth or a buzzard capable of forming the mountains and valleys. It is unclear how a woman could give birth every seven days and then change her gestation to a year (presumably actually around nine months). The creation of the sun after the Earth is also not consistent with scientific evidence.

Apache

According to Apache mythology, there was nothing. There was no Earth, Sun, or people and only darkness everywhere[cxvi]. Then a thin, yellow and white disc appeared in the sky with a small man with a white beard sitting on the disk. He was called the Creator, the One Who Lives Above. He created light. He then created a girl by putting the sweat from his head onto his hands, rubbed them together and thrust them forward. The Girl appeared on a cloud. He then wiped his face and rubbed his hands together and flung them forward and this created the Sun God and Small Boy. Now there were four gods: Creator, Girl, Sun God, and Small Boy. The cloud, where they were, was too crowded, so the Creator made the galaxy, including the big dipper, wind, clouds, and lightning. All four gods shook hands, combined their sweat, and it created a ball. Each god kicked the ball, which enlarged it and this created the Earth[cxvii]. The Creator told wind to go inside the ball and blow it up. The Creator made four giant posts to support the Earth, which were placed at the four cardinal points of the Earth and the Earth sat still. Lightning Maker brought two girls and a boy, which had no eyes, ear, hair, mouths, noses, teeth, fingers, or toes. The Sun God had a sweathouse built in which were four stones were heated by a fire inside the sweathouse. The two girls and boy were put inside the sweathouse and once they came out the Creator shook hands with them giving them eyes, ear, hair, mouths, noses, teeth, fingers, and toes.

This story of creation is not consistent with our scientific understanding of the origin of the Universe, Earth, or life. It is unclear where the Creator came from. In this scenario, apparently, one god can create another god. There is no evidence of giant posts to support the Earth and the Earth has no evidence of being inflated by wind. If it were inflated by wind, one would expect the Earth to be hollow, which it is not.

Iroquois

Apparently, there are several versions of the Iroquois creation story[cxviii]. The following is one of the versions.

Before the formation of the Earth, the area above the sky was inhabited by Superior Beings over whom the Great Spirit presided[cxix]. The daughter of the Great Spirit, Sky Woman, became pregnant by an illicit connection after which the Great Spirit tossed his daughter away. Land is created after Big Toad scoops up mud from the bottom of the sea in an effort to save Sky Woman after she falls from the sky. The mud is spread on the back of Big Turtle. The land begins to grow until it is the size of North America. Sky Woman steps onto the land and sprinkles dust into the sky. The dust becomes the moon, stars, and Sun. Sky Woman has a daughter, who is received by a middle-aged man. The daughter gave birth to twin sons, Sapling and Flint, who create of the remainder of the Earth. The daughter died in childbirth and the twins were raised by Sky Woman. Sapling brings into the world all that is good (plants, animals, and rivers), while Flint aims to destroy Sapling's good creation. The two get into a fight and Flint is defeated but doesn't die. Flint's anger is manifested into the form of a volcano.

The origin of the Great Spirit and the Superior Beings is not provided. This story has a Big Toad, which takes mud from the bottom of the sea is like the beetle in the Cherokee creation story. The amount of matter in the Universe is much greater than could be derived from taking dust from the Earth and dispersing it. Recall that the Earth is one planet among many billions in our galaxy.

Xingu (Indigenous Indians - Brazil)[cxx]

The primordial making of humans, according to upper Xingu mythology, was the work of a craftsman or creator who gave life to wooden logs placed in a seclusion compartment, by blowing tobacco smoke over them. Thus, were created the first women, among whom was the mother of the twins, Sun and Moon, archetypes and authors of present-day humanity[cxxi]. In homage to this woman, the first festival of the dead was celebrated, which is the most important festival of the Upper Xingu and which consists of a re-enactment of the primordial creation, at the same time it is the privileged moment for public presentation of the young women who have recently come out of puberty seclusion. Thus, it is a ritual that ties together death and life; the girls who come out of seclusion are like the first humans, mothers of men.

Buddhism

Buddhists believe that the beginning of this world and of life is inconceivable, since they have neither beginning nor end. Buddhism has no creator god to explain the origin of the Universe[cxxii]. Instead, it teaches that everything depends on everything else. Present events are caused by past events and become the cause of future events. Indian religions often see space and time as cyclical, such that world systems come into being, survive for a time, are destroyed, and then are remade. In Buddhism, this happens naturally without the intervention of gods.

One tale told by the Buddha describes the process of recreation[cxxiii]. An old-world system has just been destroyed, and its inhabitants are reborn in a new system. In this process spirits are floating happily above the Earth, luminescent and without form, name, or sex. The world in the early stages is without light or land, only water. Eventually the Earth appears, and the spirits come to taste and enjoy it. Their greed causes their ethereal bodies to become solid and coarse and differentiate into male and female. As they lose their luminescence the Sun and moon come into being. Gradually the beings fall into further wicked habits, causing them and the Earth to become less pleasant. In this way, the Buddha teaches that desire, greed, and attachment not only cause suffering for people but also cause the world to be as it is.

The wheel of life depicts the Buddhist Universe. The wheel itself is a circle, symbolizing the endless cycle of existence and suffering. In the middle of the wheel are the Three Fires of greed, ignorance and hatred, often represented by a rooster, a pig, and a snake. These are the cause of all suffering and are shown linked together, biting each other's tails, reinforcing each other. In the next circle out, souls are shown ascending and descending according to their karma. The next ring out is composed of six segments showing the six realms: gods, humans and Titans above and hungry ghosts, animals and those tortured in hell below. The outer ring shows twelve segments called nidanas, illustrating the Buddhist teaching of the chain of causes of suffering. The twelve nidanas[cxxiv] are:

1. Fundamental ignorance
2. Formation
3. Consciousness
4. Name and form
5. Sense faculties
6. Contact
7. Feeling or sensation
8. Craving or thirst
9. Clinging or grasping
10. Worldly existence
11. Birth or becoming
12. Old age and death

Wheel of Life[cxxv]

While it is true that present events are influenced by past events and become the cause of future events, the story of creation as described by Buddha is not consistent with a scientific explanation of the origin of the Universe and mankind. There is no evidence of the existence of hungry ghosts, a Titan World, heaven, or hell. The human world is coexistent with the animal world. While it is true that our matter is recycled into other beings, there is no evidence of spiritual reincarnation.

Zoroastrianism

According to the Zoroastrian story of creation, Ahura Mazda existed in light and goodness above, while Angra Mainyu existed in darkness and ignorance below[cxxvi]. They have existed independently of each other for all time, and manifest contrary substances. Ahura Mazda created seven abstract heavenly beings called Amesha Spentas, who support him and represent beneficent aspects, along with numerous lesser beings.

The six Amesha Spentas are[cxxvii]:
- Vohu Manah - Good mind and good purpose
- Asha Vahishta - Truth and righteousness
- Spenta Ameraiti - Holy devotion, serenity and loving kindness
- Khashathra Vairya - Power and just rule
- Hauravatat - Wholeness and health
- Ameretat - Long life and immortality

Ahura Mazda created the floating, egg-shaped Universe in two parts: first the spiritual and then 3,000 years later, the physical[cxxviii]. Ahura Mazda created Gayomard, the archetypical perfect man and the first bull. He materialized sacred fire that would serve as his own symbol upon the Earth with the ability to purify, sanctify, and create order and harmony.

While Ahura Mazda created the Universe, Gayomard, and the bull; Angra Mainyu created demons, evil lesser beings, and noxious creatures such as snakes, ants, and flies. Angra Mainyu is the originator of death and all that is evil. Angra Mainyu invaded the Universe through the base of the sky inflicting Gayomard and the bull with suffering and death. However, the evil forces were trapped in the Universe and could not retreat. The dying Gayomard and the bull emitted seeds. From the bull's seed grew all beneficial plants and animals of the world, and from the man's seed grew a plant whose leaves became the first human couple. Humans struggle in a two-fold Universe trapped with evil. The evils of this physical world are not products of an inherent weakness but are a product of Angra Mainyu's attack on creation. Angra Mainyu turned the flat, peaceful, and always lighted world into a mountainous, violent place that is half night.

In Zoroastrianism, the Universe (with both spiritual and physical components) and mankind are divinely created. This is similar to Judeo-Christian religions. Other beings are created by either a good or a bad God. The concept of competing gods or supernatural creatures of good and evil are a common theme in some other religions such as in the case of God and the devil in Christianity or Maat (harmony or order) and Isfet (chaos or violence) in ancient Egyptian beliefs. This concept is in opposition to the Bahá'í Faith that asserts that evil is non-existent and that evil is merely the lack of good, just as cold is the state of no heat, and darkness is the state of no light[cxxix].

Hinduism

The Hindu texts do not provide a single account of creation. There are a range of theories of the creation of the world, some of which are contradictory[cxxx]. The Rigveda mentions a myth whereby creation arises out of the dismemberment of a cosmic being (the Purusha[cxxxi]) who is sacrificed by the gods.

The Nasadiya Sukta[cxxxii] of the Rigveda indicates that the gods came into being after the world's creation, and nobody knows when the world first came into being.

> "Who really knows, who can declare. When it started or where from? And where will the creation end? Seekers and sought entered later and so who knows when all this manifested? That one, out of which the creation came may hold the reins or not, perceiving all from above, that one alone knows the beginning – may not know too."

According to Hindu philosophy, the Universe never came into being at some particular point, but has always been, will always be, but is in perpetually flux. Space and time are of cyclical nature. This Universe is simply the current one, which is in flux and constantly changing. When it finally ceases to manifest, a new one will arise. The birth of the Universe is followed by the life of the Universe and the destruction of the Universe. Many Hindu texts mention the cycle of creation and destruction.

The Brihadaranyaka Upanishad[cxxxiii] states that in the beginning only the Aham (self or soul) existed as the Purusha. Feeling lonely, the Purusha divided itself into two parts: male and female.

> "In the beginning, this universe was the self (Viraj) alone, in the shape of a person. He reflected and saw nothing else but His self. He first said: "I am He." Therefore, He came to be known by the name I (Aham). Hence, even now, when a person is addressed, he first says: "It is I," and then says whatever other name he may have. And because He, before (purva) the whole group of aspirants, burnt (aushat) all evils, therefore He is called Purusha. He who knows this verily burns up him who wishes to be Viraj in advance of him.
>
> He was afraid. Therefore, people still are afraid when alone. He thought: "Since there is nothing else but Myself, what am I afraid of?" Thereupon His fears were gone; for what was there to fear? Assuredly, it is from a second entity that fear arises.
>
> He was not at all happy. Therefore, a person even today is not happy when alone. He desired a mate. He became the size of a man and wife in close embrace. He divided this body into two. From that division arose husband (pati) and wife (patni). Therefore, as Yajnavalkya said, the body before one accepts a wife is one half of oneself, like the half of a split pea. Therefore, this space is indeed filled by the wife. He was united with her. From that union, human beings were born.
>
> She reflected: "How can he unite with me after having produced me from himself? Well, let me hide myself." She became a cow, the other (Manu) became a bull and was united with her; from that union cows were born. The one became a mare, the other became a stallion; the one became a she ass, the other became a he ass and was united with her; from that union, one-hoofed animals were born. The one became a she goat, the other became a he

goat; the one became a hew, the other became a ram and was united with her; from that union goats and sheep were born. Thus, indeed, he produced everything that exists in pairs, down to the ants.

The Shatapatha Brahmana states that originally, there was nothing. Death was enveloping everything. The current human generation descends from Manu, the only man who survived a great deluge. He was warned of the flood by the Matsya, fish avatar of Vishnu, and built a boat that carried the Vedas, Manu's family, and the seven sages to safety, helped by Matsya[cxxxiv]. This legend is similar to the other flood legends, such as the story of the Noah's Ark mentioned in the Bible and the Quran, and the flood myth in Gilgamesh.

The nature of Purusha is unclear. The cyclical nature of the Universe is potentially consistent with some scientific theories related to the big bang expanding and contracting Universe. Otherwise the explanation for the origin of mankind is not a scientific explanation.

Discussion

While the explanations provided by some of the religions for the origin of the Universe are interesting, they generally do not have scientific credibility. These explanations that involve a God or gods try to explain the unknown by using supernatural processes. More suspect, these stories of origin place humans as key creations opposed to merely intermediate species in a long history of evolution. While there are unique aspects of humans, there is more commonality of humans to other species than differences including some aspects that are often considered unique to mankind such as speech (i.e. elephants and whales), tool making[cxxxv], and self-awareness.[cxxxvi]

Science explains the origin of the Universe in the big bang theory. This explanation is that the Universe is the product of a singularity or point of high density, high temperature. This singularity has been tending toward disorder from the time of the generation of the Universe. The Universe is expanding, and all matter is a product of the conversion of this singularity. Life on Earth is a product of evolution. While the details of how the first lifeform originated are not completely understood, fossilized microorganisms have been found in rocks as old as 3.4 billion years[cxxxvii]. The Miller-Urey experiment provides some insight into how amino acids (possible building blocks for lifeforms) many have been formed. Some claim that life on Earth is much younger (thousands of years instead of billions) but such claims are unfounded based on well proven methods of dating such as radiometric dating.

While the scientific explanation for the origin of the Universe has significant data to support it, it ultimately has an unanswered question of where the singularity came from. The answer to this question is equally unanswered as is the question of where God or gods came from. While this question may be unanswered, it is easily seen that some religious groups provide explanations for the origin of the Universe and mankind that are based on mythology and are not consistent with science[cxxxviii].

What is the purpose of life?

Another common question that religions often try to address is "What is the purpose of life?" This question assumes that there is a purpose to life and that by understanding this purpose one can decide how to live or attempt to live life in a method consistent with this purpose.

Judaism

According to the tradition of Judaism, the purpose of life is to serve God, to keep the Torah, to avoid sin; and to pass the myriad tests which are sent our way, by properly using our free will (Deuteronomy 31:15-20)[cxxxix]. Also, the purpose of life according to the teachings of Judaism is to help HaShem (The Creator) in completing the creation of the world by making the world a better place.

Christianity

Many Christians claim that the purpose of life is to do the will of God. This begins with becoming a Christian. To determine the will of God one would need to obtain communication with God. Some claim that they can determine the will of God by reading the Bible and through prayer. Some claim to see signs or events in their lives that give them insight into the will of God. Since most people do not claim to have audible communication from God, it is difficult to know the exact will of God for any specific person in any specific situation. There are principles outlined in the Bible and by teachers of the Bible that might guide a person's decisions. There are many topics that are not addressed in the Bible. Some teachers of the Bible claim that a purpose of Christians is to witness to unbelievers so that as many as possible will be saved and go to heaven. This purpose is often connected with the Great Commission (Matthew 28:18-20). This may be part of the related purpose[cxl] of becoming "conformed to the likeness of his son" (Romans 8:29) and "to do good works, which God prepared in advance for us to do" (Ephesians 2:10).

Hinduism

According to Hinduism, the purpose of life is to achieve Dharma, Artha, Kama, and Moksha[cxli]. Each of these achievements are explained below.

1. Dharma[cxlii] is the moral law governing conduct. It means to act morally and ethically throughout one's life. Dharma also has a secondary aspect, since Hindus believe that they are born in debt to the Gods and other human beings, Dharma calls for Hindus to repay this debt. The five different debts are as follows[cxliii]:

    - debt to the Gods for their blessings
    - debt to ancestors and teachers
    - debt to guests
    - debt to mankind

- debt to cosmic elements (nature)

2. Artha[cxliv] refers to wealth and prosperity in one's life. Immoderate pursuit of wealth would lead to undesirable and ruinous excesses, artha must always be regulated by the superior aim of dharma.
3. Kama[cxlv] can be defined as pleasure. The Hindu God of love is named Kama. From this name comes the ancient guide to expression of love, the Kamasutra.
4. Moksha[cxlvi] is enlightenment. This is the most difficult meaning of life to achieve. Moksha may take an individual just one lifetime to accomplish or it may take several. It is considered the most important meaning of life and offers such rewards as liberation from reincarnation, self-realization, enlightenment, and unity with God.

Buddhism

In Buddhism, the primary purpose of life is to end suffering[cxlvii]. Buddha taught that we suffer because we strive after things that do not give lasting happiness. We try to hold on to things such as friends, health, and material things, that do not last, and this causes sorrow. Buddha did not deny that there are things in life that give joy, but he pointed out that none of them last and our attachment to them only causes more suffering. His teachings were focused on this problem and its solution. Buddhism teaches the importance of recognizing the impermanence of all things and freeing oneself from attachment to them. This will decrease suffering and eventually end the cycle of rebirth. These teachings are expressed in the Four Noble Truths and the Eightfold Path.

Four Noble Truths[cxlviii]
1. Suffering - Life involves suffering
2. Cause of Suffering - The cause of suffering is craving and ignorance

3. End of Suffering - Suffering can end because our inability to see things clearly is temporary
4. The Path - By living ethically, practicing meditation, and developing wisdom, we can follow the path of Buddha to enlightenment and freedom from suffering

Noble Eightfold Path[cxlix]
1. Right understanding or view
2. Right intent – urges us to decide what our heart wants
3. Right speech
4. Right action or conduct, includes not to kill, steal, lie, to avoid sexual misconduct, and not to take drugs or other intoxicants
5. Right livelihood
6. Right effort – cultivation of enthusiasm and a positive attitude
7. Right mindfulness – aware of the moment
8. Right concentration - meditative absorption

Together these form the foundation of belief for all branches of Buddhism, which emphasizes the purpose and methodology of ending suffering.

Islam

To a Muslim the purpose of life is to worship God under His conditions[cl]. Worshipping Allah is done by accepting Allah's will over one's own will. The act of worshipping, thanking, and extolling Allah on His Conditions is the Muslim's purpose of one's existence.

> "And I did not create the Jinn and mankind except to worship Me..." Quran, 51:56-58[cli].

Islam teaches that life is only a trial for the individual to show their true nature.

> "[He] who created death and life to test you [as to] which of you is best in deed - and He is the Exalted in Might, the Forgiving." Quran 67:2.

Death is not an ending but a beginning of the final and lasting life. This life is a preparation for the afterlife. Muslims are required to observe righteousness in their daily life, based on Quranic teachings, like eating halal food, wearing modest clothing, performing prayers, giving alms because they are to live for God alone. Thus, obedience to the will of Allah by obeying His will is the purpose of life for Muslims.

Shintoism

Shintoism places life within a world of spirituality and kami who turn away evil force and provide protection, if worshiped with respect and honor[clii]. Shintoism connects the Japanese to their land and their ancestral past. Shintoists follow in the way of their ancestors, treating the world as a spiritual place. Their purpose is to seek simplicity, be one with the world, to be in peace within the world, and to have self-discovery enabling them to reach their potential[cliii].

Wicca

Wiccans have varied beliefs regarding the purpose of life. Some claim that the purpose of life is to seek reunion with the Divine[cliv]. Everyone is created as a unique gift to the world, with special talents to offer. To refuse to use those talents is to deny one's reason for being and to let everyone down. Many Wiccans seek to cultivate a set of eight virtues: mirth, reverence, honor, humility, strength, beauty, power, and compassion.

Discussion

The purpose of life as outlined in religion is usually to live life in a manner consistent with the will of their God or Gods. Largely the purposes are to worship God and to behave according to the teachings of the religion. These actions will then influence the outcome of the persons future life.

Some people find purpose, either in addition to religious goals or outside of religion, through the generation of works of art or accomplishments. Others consider their purpose in terms of having led a life that they consider to have had some positive impact on society.

Science tells us that we are the product of our parents through the sexual process and that we carry genetic information for the preservation of our species. For the most part, we tend to try to maintain life and to promote the life of our offspring or relatives. This may impart some purpose of individuals to continue their gene pool. In some cases, individuals perform what can be considered altruistic behavior, which involves danger or death to themselves to save the lives of their others. Usually, this is for the family, tribe, or nation. As the relationship becomes more distant the genetic value of this altruism potentially decreases. This effort to pass on genes through offspring may meet a short-term goal of species preservation but it is unlikely to ultimately meet this goal in the long-term, which is explained later.

Another look at our existence is that humans serve as reservoirs for microbes. We may in some sense be vehicles for the preservation of certain types of microbial life. Thus, we serve as convenient containers and food sources for these microbes. In this case, our purpose has little to do with us and much more about preservation of microbes. This purpose may not be personally satisfying but it again is a short-term goal. This theoretical purpose of existence is accurate only from the microbe's point of view, if there is such a view.

Based on our understanding of the aging of stars, the Sun in our solar system is about 4.6 billion years old. The Sun is in a process in which nuclear fusion reactions in its core fuse hydrogen into helium. The Sun will spend about another 5 billion years in this process gradually becoming hotter because the helium atoms occupy less volume than the hydrogen atoms that were fused. As the core becomes denser the Sun will become brighter. After about 5 billion years the Sun will start to turn into a red giant. This red giant will grow so large that it will engulf Mercury, Venus, and probably the Earth.

Image of what Earth may look like 5-7 billion years from now, when the Sun swells and becomes a Red Giant[clv]

Later the Sun will become a white dwarf and ultimately a black dwarf. Regardless of the details and exact timing, the Sun will ultimately destroy all life as we know it on Earth. While it is possible that mankind or some evolutionary descendent of mankind could escape this outcome, from a long-term standpoint as the entropy of the Universe continues to increase, life will ultimately be destroyed at any location. Even in the case of a cyclical big bang and collapse model, life will ultimately be destroyed.

Thus, in terms of a purpose of life, it seems likely that there is none. Each individual may generate their own goals or purpose for their life but ultimately (in the long term, as explained above) no one's life has lasting effect. This is not to imply that life is not precious, as our lifetimes are brief in relation to astronomical time. This is also not to imply that we should not have goals and find satisfaction through our achievements.

What Happens after Death?

Another important question that religions often try to address is "What happens to me after I die?"

Christianity

Christianity claims that all humans have an afterlife. The body dies and the spirit is sent to heaven or hell, ultimately reunited with a body. The dead are either put in hell or in heaven for eternity. Catholics believe in a place or state of temporary punishment for Christians who died with unconfessed sin, which is called purgatory, but ultimately all people are destined to either heaven or hell. Protestants do not believe in purgatory (essentially a place or state where Christians with unconfessed sin can pay for these sins by punishment) but instead believe that only Christ can pay for the sins of the world, and after death people will be sent to heaven or hell permanently[clvi].

The Bible describes heaven as a highly desirable eternal destination and hell as an extremely undesirable place of eternal punishment. Hell is described as a place where there is eternal pain and suffering in a burning environment sometimes referred to as the lake of fire. Although many details of what eternal beings in heaven do other than worshipping God are not provided, there is no pain or suffering in heaven[clvii]. Interestingly, hell is described as a place where God is not present. This conflicts with the concept of God being omnipresent. The extreme differences of these two final eternal destinations is stark.

> Revelation 21:1-4 "Then I saw "a new heaven and a new earth," for the first heaven and the first earth had passed away, and there was no longer any sea. I saw the Holy City, the new Jerusalem, coming down out of heaven from God, prepared as a bride beautifully dressed for her husband. And I heard a loud voice from the throne saying, "Look! God's dwelling place is now among the people, and he will dwell with them. They will be his people, and God himself will be with them and be their God. 'He will wipe every tear from their eyes. There will be no more death' or mourning or crying or pain, for the old order of things has passed away."
>
> Matthew 18:9 "And if your eye causes you to stumble, gouge it out and throw it away. It is better for you

> to enter life with one eye than to have two eyes and be thrown into the fire of hell."
>
> Matthew 25:46 "Then they will go away to eternal punishment, but the righteous to eternal life."
>
> Jude 1:7 "In a similar way, Sodom and Gomorrah and the surrounding towns gave themselves up to sexual immorality and perversion. They serve as an example of those who suffer the punishment of eternal fire."

It is difficult to understand how any human is justly to suffer pain for eternity. One might ask, "What kind of God would torment any human being for eternity?" It seems that an all-powerful, all-knowing God could prevent His creations from going to hell, since He is the one who made hell, people, and the rules. If one were to postulate that preventing people from going to hell would take away their freedom or free will, it still stands to reason that God could have either prevented the existence of hell or made a different rule for being condemned eternally to hell.

Islam

Muslims believe in the Day of Judgment, heaven, and hell. A person's ultimate destiny, whether it is heaven or hell, depends on the degree to which that person intended and acted as God desired, with justice and mercy toward others.

> "As for him who desires the worldly pleasures, We swiftly provide in this world whatever We will to whomever We please. Then we assign to him Hell in which he shall burn despised and rejected. As for him who desires the hereafter, strives for it as he should, and is a true believer, it is such people whose efforts shall be appreciated by Allah. Each group will receive its share from the bounty of your Lord. And the bounty of your Lord is not limited" (Surah 17:18-20)[clviii]

While it is impossible to know with certainty who will go to heaven and hell, believers, who had faith in the revelations that God sent through his prophets and lived according to those revelations, may hope for heaven. It is believed that some non-believers can attain paradise by God's grace and mercy.

At the end of time, all people will be rewarded or punished according to how well they followed the instructions contained in God's revelations to his prophets. God will resurrect the dead, and each person will be judged directly by Allah according to his or her intentions and deeds. Islam teaches that God is more merciful than he is wrathful. Each person's deeds will be weighed in a balance, and if the evil deeds outweigh the good deeds, the person will be condemned to the eternal flame. If the good deeds outweigh the evil deeds, then the person will be rewarded with paradise. The Quran says that each person receives a book that contains an account of all his or her deeds, which determines their eternal destiny.

> That Day mankind will proceed in scattered groups that they may be shown their deeds. So, whosoever does good equal to the weight of an atom (or a small ant), shall see it. And whosoever does evil equal to the weight of an atom (or a small ant), shall see it. Whoever has done an atom's weight of good shall meet with its reward and whoever has done an atom's weight of evil shall meet with its consequences. (Surah 99:6-8)[clix]

Similar to the God of Christianity as discussed above, one might ask, "What kind of God would send any human being to eternal suffering because their deeds were not good enough?" Allah as with the God of Christianity had the power to prevent this and He is the one who made hell and decided to condemn his own creations.

Hinduism

Hindus believe in the rebirth and reincarnation of souls. Souls are considered immortal and imperishable. A soul is part of a of the being, which is subject to the impurities of attachment, delusion, and laws of karma[clx]. Death is a resting period during which the soul recuperates, reassembles its resources, adjusts its course, and returns again to the Earth to continue its journey. Death is a temporary cessation of physical activity, a means of recycling the resources and energy and an opportunity for the being to reenergize itself, and plan for the next phase of life. After death, a person can either be reborn and experience life once again or be liberated from the cycle of rebirth (the path of Brahman)[clxi]. The path of Brahman is achieved by rituals, gaining meditative knowledge, and love for God and is the route to salvation.

Each life experience on Earth and each incarnation of the soul offers the being an opportunity to learn and overcome its blemishes so that it can become whole. The soul needs to be born multiple times until it overcomes its state of delusion, achieves the state of equanimity, and realizes its completeness. The Bhagavad Gita says:

> "For whatever objects a man thinks of at the final moment, when he leaves the body - that alone does he attain, O son of Kunti, being ever absorbed in the thought thereof."

The last thought of the dying person inevitably reflects his inmost desire. When a person dies, their soul along with some residual consciousness leaves the body and goes to another world and returns again after spending some time there. What happens after the soul leaves the body and before it reincarnates again is a mystery.

In Hinduism when one dies the soul has a temporary rest until it becomes active again in a new human or creature. While it is scientifically correct that the matter of the body is recycled and potentially incorporated into another human or creature, this is significantly different than a soul being recycled. As there is no scientific evidence of a soul (using the meaning of a separate spiritual entity that lives forever), there is no evidence of rebirth of the soul. There are people, especially in Hindu society, which claim to be reborn. While many of these people are likely sincere, they are influenced by their imagination and beliefs. Subjects can learn to develop past-life identities that are consistent with the expectations of their therapist or hypnotist.

Dr. Ian Stevenson, University of Virginia School of Medicine, Department of Psychiatry, spent his career studying reincarnation, near-death experiences, out-of-body experiences, after-death communications, deathbed visions, and altered states of consciousness[clxii]. After 40 years of research, investigating approximately 3,000 cases of children around the world who recalled past lives, his conclusion was that there was "absence of any evidence of a physical process by which a personality could survive death and transfer to another body."

Buddhism

Buddhism teaches that we will all pass away eventually as a part in the natural process of birth, aging, and death. Thus, we should keep in mind the impermanence of life. In Buddhism, death is not the end of life, it is the end of the body we inhabit in this life, but our spirit will remain and see attachment to a new body and new life. Although there are some differences[clxiii] in Buddhist beliefs regarding the afterlife (Mahayana School versus Theravada School), they agree that the realm of reincarnation is a result of the past and the accumulation of positive and negative actions.

The supreme aim of Buddhism is to obtain nirvana or enlightenment. If a person does not obtain nirvana, they are to be reborn in one of six realms, which are[clxiv]:

- Heaven – there are 37 different levels of heaven
- Human Life – conditions of birth are affected by past karma
- Asura - demi-gods consumed by jealousy
- Hungry ghosts - spiritual realm of those who committed excessive amounts of evil deeds, obsessed with finding food and drink
- Animal – where humans are reborn if they killed animals or committed other evil acts
- Hell - place were beings born experience a constant state of searing pain

The realm to which a person is reborn is dependent on the severity of their karmic actions. Buddhists believe one does not remain in any one place indefinitely. In Buddhism, life does not end. It continues in other forms that are the result of accumulated karma.

The Buddhist description of what happens after death has some similarities to Hinduism in that the soul is recycled and can be placed in humans or animals. It also has some aspects similar to that of Christianity/Islam, in that the eternal soul can be destined to heaven or hell, albeit temporarily.

Discussion

One of the main problems of mankind and of all life (with perhaps some rare exceptions as in the case of the immortal jellyfish[clxv] and regenerating flatworms[clxvi]) is that death appears inevitable.

Turritopsis dohrnii - The immortal jellyfish[clxvii]

Even immortal beings will be destroyed based on the ultimate destiny of the Universe (discussed earlier). While it is personally desirable to obtain eternal life, it does not appear achievable, at least in a physical sense. Many people try to leave a legacy in terms of progeny or works (i.e. art, literature, architecture, invention) but this does not change the fact that the individual will die. Also, based on our understanding of the Universe, all life on Earth will eventually be destroyed and the Universe is continuing toward a state of disorder[clxviii].

Religion tries to address this concern of eventual death by providing a hope for the spirit or soul of everyone to live forever. Additionally, some religions provide for an opportunity to live forever in a better state (i.e. heaven, paradise). Let us examine whether there is any basis for such a belief.

It is seen that our bodies age and that we eventually die. The materials of the body are generally recycled for incorporation into the Earth or other beings. We see the physical decomposition and recycling of the material body after death. The materials of the body are digested by microbes and become components of other beings, if they are consumed. The process of the input of matter into the body, reconfiguration, and loss of matter are an ongoing process during life. If we examine the world around us, we notice that for all animals the basis of life requires the death of others. This process of the consumption of biological matter by other forms of life for existence is sometimes referred to as the food chain.

Example of Food Chain[clxix]

Even plants, which usually do not kill other forms of life for sustenance benefit from the decay of other forms of life and are in a constant battle against other plants and animals for continuance of their existence (both individually and as a species).

Our existence is dependent on killing and animals are specialized for the ability to hunt and kill other forms of life. For example, anteaters have elongated snouts with a thin tongue, no teeth, and curved foreclaws, which enables them to tear open mounds of ant and termites and eat them. It is apparent that some species are dependent on the existence of specific types of other life for food. Humans require carbohydrates, protein, fats, minerals, and vitamins to maintain health. Cellular function depends on use of the energy stored in organic molecules such as carbohydrate (including sugars), fats, and proteins.

Many species have evolved (even in the short term) to enable them to adapt to their predatory environments. One might ask, "What kind of God would develop such a system, where life of one entity is dependent on the killing of another?" A general answer provided by Christianity to this question is that this system (based on death) is blamed on sin.

> "but of the tree of the knowledge of good and evil you shall not eat, for in the day that you eat of it you shall surely die." Genesis 2:17
>
> "By the sweat of your brow you will eat your food until you return to the ground, since from it you were taken; for dust you are and to dust you will return." Genesis 3:19
>
> "For the wages of sin is death, ..." Romans 6:23a
>
> "By one man sin entered the world, and death by sin, and so death passed upon all men, for that all have sinned" Romans 5:12

This answer only temporarily deflects the blame, since God is ultimately responsible for all His creations. If God is omniscient and omnipotent, He would have the knowledge and power to make His universe work however He wanted it to work. Thus, God would have had the option of never created such beings or could have kept such events from occurring. So, either there is no God or there is a God who allowed the current system of life depending on the death of others (i.e. the food chain). It is worthy of reflection on what kind of God would create such a system. While some may consider this "circle of life" as an inevitable reality, in truth the system is brutal and ultimately leads to the death and destruction of all individuals. This system leads to evolution, which depends the weaker mutations dying and stronger mutations surviving.

The proposition that religions often put forth is that there is an unseen part of each of us that continues to live after the body dies. This proposition is considered to only be true for humans and is not the case for other forms of life in religions such as Christianity, Judaism, and Islam, whereas animals have souls in religions such as Hinduism and Sikhism[clxx].

Such an entity theoretically continues to exist after death of the body. The concept of the existence of an invisible, undetectable spirit or soul is encountered in folklore, myths, and religions, which are typically unreliable sources of information. Folklore, myths, and religions are often based on exaggerations of the truth and are usually factually incorrect. While it is basically impossible to prove the non-existence of souls or spirits, there is no scientific evidence for a spirit or soul. Although it may be possible to prove non-existence in special situations, such as showing that a container does not contain certain items, one cannot prove universal or absolute non-existence. The proof of existence must come from those who make the claims[clxxi]. Without proof, evidence, or at least some logical rationale for the theory, it remains an unsubstantiated claim.

It is an interesting question of when such a soul or spirit (eternal non-physical entity) would be generated. If only humans or animals have spirits, then is this entity generated when the egg and sperm are united (fertilization) as a zygote or would this happen later, after implantation of the fertilized egg, when there is brain activity, or perhaps when the fetus is viable outside the uterus? Also, is it unclear how is a spirit generated and what is a spirit made of if it is immaterial.

Religions through the concept of an eternal soul or spirit attempt to provide a hope to alleviate concerns about the eventual death that we all are going to experience. Some consider that living a life with knowledge that there is no afterlife renders them without a purpose for continuing to live. In reality, understanding that there is no afterlife can provide an accurate description of life and death that encourages the appreciation of life due to its brevity and fragility.

There are accounts by people that have had near death experiences (NDE)s. The information from these individuals is of questionable value because their experiences are likely a result of effects of anoxia of the brain. Accounts of seeing a light and tunnels may have physiological explanations related to hallucinations caused by decreased oxygen to the brain[clxxii]. Neuroscientists Olaf Blanke and Sebastian Dieguez (2009)[clxxiii], from the in Switzerland propose a brain based model with two types of NDEs:

- "type 1 NDEs are due to bilateral frontal and occipital, but predominantly right hemispheric brain damage affecting the right temporal parietal junction and characterized by out of body experiences, altered sense of time, sensations of flying, lightness, vection [sensation of movement of the body in space] and flying[clxxiv]"

- "type 2 NDEs are also due to bilateral frontal and occipital, but predominantly left hemispheric brain damage affecting the left temporal parietal junction and characterized by feeling of a presence, meeting and communication with spirits, seeing of glowing bodies, as well as voices, sounds, and music without vection"

They suggest that damage to the bilateral occipital cortex may lead to visual features of NDEs such as seeing a tunnel or lights, and "damage to unilateral or bilateral temporal lobe structures such as the hippocampus and amygdala" may lead to emotional experiences, memory flashbacks or a life review. They conclude that future neuroscientific studies are likely to reveal the neuroanatomical basis of NDEs, which will lead to the demystification of the subject without needing paranormal explanations. There is a strong desire for continuance of life after death but that which is desired versus reality may differ.

Chapter 3 Purpose of Religions

Let us now examine some of the purposes of religions. It is logical that religions would likely not exist if they had no benefit, at least at some point in human history. We will discuss whether religions may have conferred some evolutionary advantage such as social solidarity, may have emerged as a method to deal with psychological issues such as causation, or have some other purposes. Some other potential purposes of religion such as to provide a purpose to life or provide hope for an afterlife have been discussed previously and will not be reiterated.

Getting What You Want During Life

During our lives, we encounter favorable and unfavorable events, such as good or bad harvests, sickness, healing, death, and births. It is sometimes unclear why things go well or poorly and both types of events are encountered by all people. Since many of these things are or appear to be outside our control, some people conclude that a God (or gods) is (are) in control of these events. If one were able to influence the God or gods, then perhaps things would go better. Such appears to be the origin of rituals and/or prayers. These rituals tend to continue even in the absence of effect, as one can never be sure if the reason for failure is due to the worshipper's fault or because of the God's or gods' will. One might ask whether such an action would ever change God's will; if God's will is predetermined, as is taught by the protestant reformer John Calvin. If this were the case, such actions might be pointless because God was going to do what He wanted regardless of any action of the worshippers[clxxv].

Moslem Praying[164]

The Inuit believe that all things have a spirit or soul, including humans. According to a customary Inuit saying, "The great peril of our existence lies in the fact that our diet consists entirely of souls." Since all beings possess souls like those of humans, killing an animal is like killing a person[clxxvi]. Once the soul or spirit of the dead animal or human is liberated, it is free to take revenge. According to the Inuit, the spirit of the dead can only be placated by obedience to custom, avoiding taboos, and performing the right rituals.

The Mayans offered sacrifice to establish and renew relationships with the other world. In contemporary sacrificial rites, there is an overall emphasis on the sprinkling of blood[clxxvii]. In the pre-Spanish past, sacrifice usually consisted of animals such as deer, dog, quail, turkey, and fish. On exceptional occasions, such as accession to the throne, severe illness of the ruler, a royal burial, or drought and famine, sacrifices included adult human beings and/or children. Eating of the sacrifice was common, but ritual cannibalism appears to have been rare. Mayan rituals included bloodletting in which the earlobes, tongues, and foreskins were cut with sharp knives and the blood fell on paper strips that were burnt.

Mayan Sacrifice by Heart Removal[clxxviii]

For the Aztecs, sacrifice and death was necessary for the continued existence of the world. Likewise, each part of life had one or more deities associated with it and these had to be paid their dues. Gods were given sacrificial offerings of food, flowers, effigies, and quail. The larger the effort required of the God, the greater the sacrifice had to be. Blood was fed to the Gods to keep the sun from falling. For some of the most important rites, a priest would offer his own blood, by cutting his ears, arms, tongue, thighs, chest, or genitals, or offer a human life. Human sacrifice was practiced throughout the Aztec empire, although the exact figures are unknown. At Tenochtitlan [Mexico] between 10,000 and 80,400 persons were sacrificed over the course of four days for the dedication of the Great Pyramid in 1487.

Excavations of the offerings in the main temple have provided some insight into the process, but the dozens of remains excavated are far short of the thousands of sacrifices recorded by eyewitnesses and other historical accounts. The practice of human sacrifice was widespread in Mesoamerican and South American cultures. Human sacrifice was a complex ritual. Every sacrifice had to be planned from the type of victim to the specific ceremony needed for the God. The sacrificial victims were usually warriors but were sometimes slaves, depending upon the needed ritual. The higher the rank of the warrior the more valuable they were as a sacrifice. The victims would take on the persona of the God that they were to be sacrificed for. The victims would be housed, fed, and dressed accordingly, potentially for up to a year.

When the sacrificial day arrived, the victims would participate in the specific ceremonies of the God. These ceremonies were used to exhaust the victim so that he would not struggle during the ceremony. Then priests performed the sacrifice usually at the top of a pyramid. The victim would be laid upon the table, held down and then have his heart cut out.

There are known examples of the formation of religions considered as cargo cults[clxxix] in Melanesia and New Guinea. Natives on these islands developed rituals in an attempt to influence the outcome of events to favor them. They wanted the return of American World War II soldiers to their islands to bring them desired goods. Symbols associated with Christianity and modern Western society tended to be incorporated into their rituals. Examples of cargo cult activity include the setting up of mock airstrips, airports, airplanes, and attempted construction of Western goods, such as radios made of coconuts and straw. The natives staged marches with sticks for rifles and use military-style insignia painted on their bodies to make them look like soldiers as rituals to be performed for the purpose of attracting the soldiers and their cargo. One cargo cult that arose in the 1930's in New Hebrides centered on a figure named John Frum.

Ceremonial cross of John Frum cargo cult,
Tanna, New Hebrides[clxxx]

There are a number of circumstances and events in life that we have little control over. Our energies are best spent in dealing the best we can with these circumstances or events. The best method for obtaining what one desires in life is to apply one's efforts to achieve these goals. Hoping for recompense or a better life in the afterlife is likely unfounded. While most religions teach that there is an afterlife, there is no evidence to support such claims[clxxxi]. Thus, expecting that one's deeds in this life will affect an outcome in an afterlife is equally unfounded. It is reasonable that one's actions in this life will affect this life. Hoping for a God or gods to change events in your favor through any means including prayer or offerings is likely pointless unless some other human intervenes in your behalf[clxxxii]. Prayer may have the effect of keeping one's desires in mind and letting others know what you desire such that they may have influence. Religions tend to provide what is likely false hope and similarly lead to the waste of human effort on pointless activities or destructive behaviors as in the case of human and animal sacrifice.

Many people within religions are often encouraged to spread their religion as a devotion to their God and they tend do so in honest ignorance of the falsity of their religion. The waste of money and time by people endeavoring to sustain and spread religion is staggering.

In some cases, the missionary efforts involve humanitarian efforts. In some cases, little of the missionary resources are actually used for beneficial efforts[clxxxiii]. There's no shortage of secular groups that feed the hungry and house the poor and fight for the underprivileged. Albeit there are in some cases in both religious and non-religious groups misuse of funds by people in those organizations. Religious people may often donate to religious charities because those groups may provide humanitarian benefit to proselytize. There is a tendency for people in these religions to not only prefer their religion to others but also to prefer their culture to that of others. Often these means that missionaries not only try to change the religion of others but also their culture, which may alienate those proselytized from their friends and family. This means that some of that money being donated is going toward spreading their faith and not actually helping other people.

Societal Control

As we have seen, religions are formed by individuals or groups. Early organized religions appear to have provided divine authority to religious leaders, a cultural bond among tribes or bands, and facilitated cooperation within the group. There are a number of examples of theocracies, where a deity is the source of authority for the government including the Pharaonic Egypt, Early Roman Empire, Mayas, Incas, Papal States, Islamic States including Iran, Central Tibetan Administration, and the Byzantine Empire[clxxxiv]. In many of these cases, the religious leaders assume the leading role in the state.

Ali Khamenei, Supreme Leader of Iran[clxxxv]
The country's leading political and religious figure.

Many religious leaders decide to revise existing religions. The initial version of Judaism (First Temple) appears to be based in part on elements of Babylonian religion. Christianity is a modified version of Judaism, and Islam is a modified version of Christianity. In the case of Joseph Smith, who formed Mormonism, he claimed to have visions, which lead him to form this revised version of Christianity. Martin Luther was a reformer and founder of Protestantism, which is a modified version of Catholicism.

Martin Luther[clxxxvi]

These new groups that are derived from the old can be unified under new leadership with revised rules and religious concepts.

One potential goal of these leaders is to form cohesiveness of the group and enable them to dictate the rules of the religion, which then often become elements of their culture. Religions provide an opportunity to justify political power through divine authority. Kingship (or any kind of absolutist power) and its close relationship to and use of religion for the purpose of legitimizing power is seen repeatedly in human history[clxxxvii]. The use of religion to justify authoritative political systems in the Middle East is seen in currently[clxxxviii].

Religions provide uniformity in society and allow the indoctrination of believers to conform to desired behaviors. Religious texts or laws can be generated by those in authority to define acceptable behavior. Those in positions of authority in the religion obtain power over the believing populace allowing them to control the people. Religion can be used to institute standardization and social order among people and make people better fit to be controlled or control others, and more likely to preserve social institutions[clxxxix]. Religion is perhaps the best and surest way to make a group of people constant and submissive. Human history is filled with examples where leaders have used religion to institute and preserve standardization of their people. Religious authority was used in ancient Egypt to enable the construction of the Pyramids and similarly in Mesopotamia for construction of temples. Throughout human history almost every time a large region adopted an official religion, one of the main motives that its leaders had for doing so was to contribute to this mass standardization of the people. During the reign of Constantine Christianity spread enabling greater uniformity of religion. The spread of Islam promoted adherence to the doctrines and laws of Islam.

Religions are also used to make financial profit and to access resources. There have been many cases in which authority has been misused by corrupt religious figures. While some religious leaders are one of the many types of leaders that sometimes use their positions to make profit unethically, there is an expectation by the believers that the leaders would be ethical based on their mission. Examples of some corrupt religious figures include[cxc]:

- Jim Bakker – Created Praise the Lord Organization – fraud and conspiracy, illegally soliciting millions of dollars from his followers
- Oral Roberts – Founder of Charismatic Movement – fraudulent solicitation of donations from followers
- Hogen Fukunaga – Founder of Ho No Hana – fraudulently gaining 150 million yen from his followers
- L. Ron Hubbard – Founder of Scientology – illegal business practices, false claims about his ability to cure physical illnesses
- David Yonggi Cho – Founder of Yoido Full Gospel Church – embezzled 13 billion won in church funds
- Jim Jones – Disciples of Christ Pastor - responsible for a mass suicide in Jonestown, Guyana
- Paul Schäfer - Former head of Chile-based Colonia Dignidad - convicted of sexually abusing 25 children
- David Koresh – Leader of Branch Davidians Religious Cult – Siege in Waco, Texas leading to death of 80 (including Koresh)
- Shoko Asahara – Founder of Aum Shinrikyo – Sarin gas attack on the Tokyo subway

Karl Marx discusses religion as the "opiate of the masses" and the significant role it plays in maintaining the status quo[cxci]. He argued that religion keeps the masses docile. The religious leader can define the way to salvation and can teach how it is possible to achieve it. Religious leaders can also rally personnel and resources to actions such as crusades or jihads.

Churches and temples have often been centers of the community where the pulpits are used to influence the actions of the congregation. Sometimes the pulpit is used to promoting or opposing political candidates. It is questionable as to whether tax-exempt organizations should be allowed to openly participate in political campaigning[cxcii]. In the United States, a group of fundamentalist Christian pastors founded an organization called the Moral Majority as a political action group, which played a significant role in the 1980 elections. Religious figures have often used their positions to preach for political and social change. Many religious leaders including Martin Luther King used the pulpit to encourage protest during segregation.

Jerry Falwell, whose founding of the Moral Majority - prominent American political organization associated with the Christian right and Republican Party[cxciii]

Some might consider religions as a means to teach and encourage moral behavior. The definition of moral behavior defined by the various religions is not consistent among each other. Many religions have influenced the legal system to incorporate their beliefs in moral behavior into law. Examples include Sharia Law in some Muslim nations including Saudi Arabia and Iran and religious laws in the U.S. including Sunday closing laws, and laws concerning abortion or homosexual conduct. There are several countries that have religious requirements for heads of state[cxciv]. Many Muslim nations require that their heads of state be held by a Muslim, including Afghanistan, Algeria, Iran, Jordan, Malaysia, Pakistan, Saudi Arabia, Syria, and Yemen. Bhutan and Thailand require their monarchies to be Buddhist and Andorra and Lebanon require heads of state to have a Christian affiliation.

Often those who make the laws are often steeped in religion, which influences their decisions. Religions are not necessary to promote morality[cxcv] and that they can corrupt moral values based on false premises. As we will discuss later, it can be seen where religious belief has encouraged cruelty, torture, and murder of others.

Religion as a Social Club

Humans are social beings and as such often seek out the companionship or friendship of others. Local congregations of various religions that meet regularly serve as an opportunity for social engagement. There tends to be a willingness for incorporating new people into these groups as they serve as possible sources of labor and money. Albeit there may be limits to the willingness to accept adherents into some religious groups, if they do not fit into the group (i.e. excommunication or disfellowship). Often these groups openly seek recruitment of seekers, non-believers, or new believers into their groups to expand their capacity. By joining a local group people can develop essentially social clubs and be involved in other people's lives. This type of social engagement can be achieved by joining secular organizations similarly.

The church, temple, or mosque serves as a means to participate with others that are largely likeminded at least in regard to religion and to have confirmation of these beliefs, even if it is a minority view in society. Larger groups often provide meetings of similarly aged attendees to meet, such as children being taught together in age separated groups. Often the teachings are aimed at the interests of the age-related group, such as religious views of dating might be taught to young adults or a single's group. The organizational structure of religious groups enables opportunity for leadership roles and training about the group's activities. Many people attend organized religious meetings as a ritual or habit but find it appealing because of the ceremonial entertainment, friendships, or acquaintances developed, and confirming rhetoric. Spending time and developing friendships with people who believe similarly reinforces the belief system and limits the ability of people to be exposed to opposing views and limits understanding of differing opinions. Similarly, some attend religious schools to develop friendships with likeminded people and potentially find mates.

While religious groups may provide an opportunity to have social interaction, this is a social group that teaches incorrect information (since there are conflicting doctrines between religions, not all information can be correct and there is significant conflict between unsubstantiated religious dogma and well supported scientific information). These groups also take time and money from their attendees that could potentially be used more productively[cxcvi,cxcvii], and often promote separateness from those that do not adhere to their beliefs. This separateness often leads to either a perception of superiority of the group or a hatred for those who do not adhere to their perceived code of conduct and beliefs. Such local groups can easily become influenced by the cultish beliefs of their leadership. This can either make the group disparate or potentially dangerous to others (i.e. ISIS) or themselves (i.e. David Koresh).

Religion as a Business

Religions enable a process of extraction of resources from the believers through tithes, donations, offerings, or fees. The money obtained from the adherents is often used to pay for salaries of employees including missionaries of the church, temple, etc. as well as advertising, programs, and maintenance. Religious leaders have created a variety of ways in which to obtain money. Often Christian organizations will tell believers that they can give money to the church to store up rewards in heaven; sort of like a bank account in heaven.

> Matthew 6:19-21 "Do not store up for yourselves treasures on earth, where moth and rust destroy, and where thieves break in and steal. But store up for yourselves treasures in heaven, where moth and rust do not destroy, and where thieves do not break in and steal. For where your treasure is, there your heart will be also....

Tithes are encouraged based on some passages in the Bible. Tithes are generally considered to be 10% of a person's income to be given to the church. The Catholic Church enabled the purchase of indulgences. Scientology charges a membership fee, course fees, and large sums of money for their books, lectures, and audio CDs. Church taxes are imposed on members of some religious organizations in Europe[cxcviii]. Similarly, the Zakat, Islamic religious tax, is one of the pillars of Islam. Some Islamic extremists use kidnapping and obtaining ransom for hostages. More extreme methods used during eras of persecution include killing people and taking their property (examples include Jewish holocaust in WWII, Christian crusades, and Islamic conquests).

Annual revenues of faith-based enterprises including churches, hospitals, schools, charities are more than $378 billion in the US[cxcix]. The Faith Counts study examined 344,894 congregations, from 236 different religious denominations (217 of them Christian, and others ranging from Shinto to Tao to Zoroastrian) in the United States. Collectively, those congregations count for about half the American population as members. The average annual income for a congregation is approximately $242,900. Most of that income comes from members' donations and dues, meaning Americans give $74.5 billion to their congregations per year.

The founder of Scientology, L Ron Hubbard, used his religion as a means to obtain power and make money for himself[cc]. For the last two years of his life, Hubbard lived in on a 160-acre ranch near Creston, California[cci].

L. Ron Hubbard, Founder of the Church of Scientology[ccii]

He repeatedly redesigned the property, spending millions of dollars remodeling the ranch house and building a quarter-mile horse race track, which reportedly was never used. He was closely involved in managing the Church of Scientology via secretly delivered orders and continued to receive large amounts of money, of which Forbes magazine estimated "at least $200 million [was] gathered in Hubbard's name through 1982." In September 1985, the Internal Revenue Service notified the Church that it was considering indicting Hubbard for tax fraud.

A number of preachers have become rich by means of funds obtained from religious adherents. The miracle crusade televangelist Benny Hinn has a net worth of 24 million dollars[cciii]. Joel Osteen, the senior pastor of Lakewood Church in Houston, Texas has a net worth of 40 million dollars. Creflo Dollar, pastor and founder of non-denominational World Changers Church International has a net worth of 27 million dollars. He owns two Rolls-Royces, a private jet, and three multimillion-dollar homes. Jim Bakker and his PTL associates sold $1,000 "lifetime memberships," which entitled buyers to a three-night stay annually at a luxury hotel at Heritage USA[cciv]. Tens of thousands of memberships were sold, but only one 500-room hotel was ever completed. Bakker sold more "exclusive partnerships" than could be accommodated, while raising more than twice the money needed to build the actual hotel. A good deal of the money went into Heritage USA's operating expenses, and Bakker kept $3.4 million in bonuses for himself.

Jim and Tammy Faye Bakker at their PTL Ministry in 1986[ccv]

Oral Roberts, an American Charismatic Christian televangelist was a founder of the Charismatic movement and the founder of Oral Roberts University[ccvi]. In January 1987, during a fundraising drive, Roberts announced to a television audience that unless he raised $8 million by that March, God would "call him home." However, the year before on Easter he had told a gathering at the Dallas Convention Center that God had instructed him to raise the money "by the end of the year" or he would die. Regardless of this new March deadline and the fact that he was still $4.5 million short of his goal, some were fearful that he was referring to suicide, given the impassioned pleas and tears that accompanied his statement. He raised $9.1 million.

While many religious leaders may not become exceedingly wealthy, many are able to obtain comfortable lifestyles through tithes and offerings from their churches.

Discussion

We have examined some purposes of religions including that religions were developed as a hopeful means of getting God or the gods to provide what they wanted, although this might require sacrifice. Religions have been and continue to be used as a means to control people and influence governments (i.e. Moral Majority and use of the pulpit for political persuasion). Religious leaders obtain power over people and can use this to obtain resources and promote their agendas. The agendas of these religious leaders vary and sometimes oppose each other. For example, some leaders promoted racial equality (Martin Luther King) while others promoted racial inequality (Wesley Swift[ccvii]). Similarly, there have been religious leaders against slavery and those that promoted slavery[ccviii]. Religions provide opportunities for social engagement and isolationism from differing opinions.

While social involvement is valuable, religious groups often encourage regular meetings to promote reinforcement of their religion. The Westminster Confession urges a strict observance of the Lord's Day as a day of rest and worship, away from "works, words, and thoughts" about "worldly employments and recreations." The whole time is to be devoted to "public and private exercises of [God's] worship, and in duties of necessity and mercy." In the United States, many "blue laws" relating to Sunday originated from this general prescription observed by American Puritans of the Reformed tradition[ccix]. Continuous indoctrination and encouragement of conformity from fellow attendees encourages little reflection on the truth of the religion or lack of truth. This continued religious input decreases opportunity for unbiased analysis of alternative world views[ccx].

We have seen that some religious leaders use their religion either to get rich or to at least make a living (usually as a parasite on the followers). Providing a hope for an eternal life encourages living one's life in a manner that is consistent with obtaining this goal, albeit there is no proof of the existence of an afterlife. Religions often define rules of behavior for obtaining eternal life in a heaven, paradise, or nirvana. This enables religions to control the behavior of the adherents to that religion. People in positions of authority within the religion can use this control to their advantage in encouraging believers to give them money and resources or to be willing to suffer or die for their religious cause. This latter enables the waging of "holy" wars and the martyrdom of believers, which will be discussed later.

Chapter 4 Validity of Religions

To determine the validity of a proposition or claim we expect evidence to support the claim. If one is to make a claim as is done in religion, the burden of proof[ccxi] is on the religion. It is not necessary to prove the non-existence of a claim because non-existence requires omniscience. For example, one might claim that yellow polka dotted aliens, leprechauns, and tooth fairies exist. It is not a sufficient proof to claim it is so, since no one has proven otherwise.

There are expectations that a claim should not be self-conflicting. The claim should also be consistent with known facts (information presented as having objective reality[ccxii]) and logic. The more evidence and its probable truth or accuracy increases the likelihood of a correct evaluation of the validity of a claim[ccxiii]. We will attempt to examine the validity of religion based on factual and scientific information available to us. Since religions disagree among each other in many aspects and some have changed over time, we will seek to determine if any of the religions or versions of that religion are true.

Group 1 – Judaism, Christianity, and Islam

To conduct this evaluation, let us examine some of the claims of various religions. First, let us examine a group of related monotheistic religions (Judaism, Christianity, and Islam).

Judaism

Key claims in Judaism are outlined in Rabbi Moses ben Maimon's (Maimonides) thirteen principles of faith[ccxiv]:
- God exists
- God is one and unique
- God is incorporeal
- God is eternal
- Prayer is to be directed to God alone and to no other
- The words of the prophets are true
- Moses' prophecies are true, and Moses was the greatest of the

prophets
- The Written Torah (first 5 books of the Bible) and Oral Torah (teachings now contained in the Talmud and other writings) were given to Moses
- There will be no other Torah
- God knows the thoughts and deeds of men
- God will reward the good and punish the wicked
- The Messiah will come
- The dead will be resurrected

Christianity

Some claims in Christianity include:
- Jesus Christ is God and was a man, born of a virgin, lived a sinless life, and died for the sins of all people
- God exists as a trinity of God the father, God the son (Jesus), and the Holy Ghost (Spirit)
- All people have sinned and destined for hell unless they accept Jesus as their savior
- Believers in Jesus Christ will go to heaven for eternity
- Non-believers in Jesus Christ will go to hell for eternity
- The Universe was created by God in seven days
- The Bible is the Word of God and is without error
- Jesus will return to Earth and will raise the dead for a final judgment

Islam

Some claims in Islam include:
- There is one God, Allah
- The Quran is the revelation of God through the Prophet Muhammad and it is protected from corruption or distortion
- In the day of judgment all people will be resurrected for God's judgment (going to either paradise or hell)
- Allah created man from a clot of blood and jinn from fire

Since these religions have some common concepts, let us examine those common concepts to examine their validity and then we will examine a few concepts that are unique.

Existence of a Creator God

God is considered to be omnipresent, omnipotent, and omniscient. God is usually considered to be an invisible spirit or at least normally not seen. To support the claim of the existence of the God of Judaism, Christianity, or Islam, we would seek some evidence of His existence. What evidence is there for the existence of God?

There are biblical references to people who were claimed to have seen God but they were supposed to have seen physical representations of God to enable direct communication[ccxv]. The veracity of these stories is impossible to determine. Some claim that we can see God in the nature, which is His creation. Although there is beauty and complexity in nature, nature is brutal with most life only able to continue by the death and consumption of other living forms. Some claim that they can hear God speak to them through circumstances or by reading scripture. The veracity of these claims is questionable, since these thoughts may not come from God.

Some claim that there is a God based on the anthropic principle, which indicates that since the Universe is specifically compatible for life as we know it, there is a creator behind such circumstances[ccxvi]. This is based on the specific location and circumstances of the Earth that makes life possible on Earth. Based on data from NASA's planet-hunting Kepler spacecraft, scientists predict that there should be an Earth-sized planet in the habitable zone of each red dwarf. The Milky Way alone may host 60 billion such planets[ccxvii,ccxviii]. One should consider that there are many planets like the Earth that could support life and that life could take different forms than is known on Earth. For example, it was not known that life could exist based on the thermal vents at the bottom of the sea. The Drake Equation has been used to estimate the number of communicating civilizations in the Universe[ccxix]. Although the equation can give a wide range of values depending on assumptions, a low estimate using NASA's star formation rates is 15,600,000 civilizations[ccxx].

Some may claim that the existence of the Universe is evidence of God. This relates to the question of where the Universe came from. While it is unclear what is the origin of all matter and energy, even in the big bang theory, this does not necessitate the existence of the creator Gods of Judaism, Christianity, or Islam.

Inerrant Scripture Written by God

Jewish fundamentalists believe that the Jewish Bible, as interpreted in the rabbinic tradition, is infallible. The Bible is claimed to be the inerrant, Word of God in fundamental Christianity. Muslims believe that some of the Bible (Torah, Psalms, and the Gospel) are a revelation from Allah but some of the Bible has become distorted, corrupted, or added. The Quran is considered the verbatim word of Allah and is considered infallible in Islam. What evidence do we have that these religious books are from God and are infallible?

Literature is normally written by humans and is the invention of these authors. The Bible is thought to have been written by a large number of individuals over centuries. Each of these authors was to have been inspired by God to write these books. The Quran was written during a period of over 20 years. A book written by an omniscient God would not be expected to have errors in it. Some people have made a close examination of the Bible and claim that there are a substantial number of inconsistencies with books of the Bible and between books of the Bible[ccxxi]. Similarly, there are a number of apparent contradictions in the Quran[ccxxii]. There are those who claim to be able to explain all contradictions, but one must judge for themselves, if the explanations are reasonable.

There are a large number of claims for supernatural events and never seen creatures in these religious books. This includes such items as the existence of angels and demons, a world-wide flood and rescue of all animal life in an ark, resurrection from the dead, virgin birth, talking animals, walls of a city falling down by virtue of a trumpet/shout, changing of water to wine, and creation of the Universe in six days. These are the types of things that are easily attributed to be the invention of people's imagination. While events in our recent known history include sometimes rare events, supernatural events have not been substantiated. There is also no credible evidence for the existence of angels or demons.

If there were a God and He wanted to provide instructions to mankind, then it would seem logical that the information should be provided at the beginning of mankind's existence (in the language of that time) and that the information would be provided in a material means that would not be able to be destroyed or distorted. This would enable all people to know God's message for all time. We know that the Hebrew Bible was written in the 10th to 6th century BCE[ccxxiii], the new testament was written between 30-100 CE[ccxxiv], and the Quran was written between 609-632 CE[ccxxv]. Thus, many people would have been born and died without any scriptures. Based on the content of the gospel, people can only be saved by belief in Jesus Christ.

One would expect that an infallible message from God would reflect the person of this God. The Bible and Quran have messages that impact the eternal destiny of people. It is interesting to consider what happens to those who never heard of Jesus and had the opportunity to accept Jesus as savior. This would include not only those in remote areas, times past, and those who are too young to understand language or such concepts. If it is the case that people become accountable after such knowledge and would be destined to heaven as a default, then it would have been better to kill them prior to any opportunity to learn or understand the gospel. Such a proposition is detestable. If they are destined for hell as a default, then God is evil in allowing them to ever have been created. Would such a God be worthy of love, devotion, or acceptance? This bears on the credibility of scriptures that provide such a doctrine of salvation.

The Existence of Heaven and Hell

Many religions have the concept of a place or state of punishment (hell) and a place or state of reward (heaven) for humans after death.

Existence of Hell

In Judaism, the place for the dead is described as Sheol, which appears to be in the Earth.

> "As he finished speaking all these words, the ground that was under them split open; and the earth opened its mouth and swallowed them and their households, and all those associated with Korah, together with their possessions. So, they and all that belonged to them went down alive to Sheol; and the earth closed over them, and they perished from the midst of the assembly. ccxxvi" Numbers 16:31-33

In the New Testament, Jesus describes hell in a parable as a place of eternal torment.

> "The time came when the beggar died and the angels carried him to Abraham's side. The rich man also died and was buried. In Hades, where he was in torment, he looked up and saw Abraham far away, with Lazarus by his side. So, he called to him, 'Father Abraham, have pity on me and send Lazarus to dip the tip of his finger in water and cool my tongue, because I am in agony in this fire.'" Luke 16:22-24 ccxxvii

The follow descriptions of hell or Jahannam are from the Quran:

> "Fear the fire, which is prepared for the disbelievers." [Quran 3: 131]

> "Verily, Allah has cursed the disbelievers and prepared for them a Blazing Fire. Dwelling therein forever, and they will find no protector or helper. [Quran 33: 64-65] ccxxviii

So, what evidence is there of hell or sheol?

One may ask, "If there is a hell or sheol, where is it?" No one has located hell in our Universe. The passage in Numbers 33 describes the Earth opening up and swallowing people, but there is no evidence of hell in the center of the Earth.

The Earth has multiple layers. The outermost layer is the crust. About 30 km below your feet is where the next layer of the Earth, the mantle, starts. The mantle makes up the majority of the interior of the Earth, and its composed of heated rock under high pressure. Inside the mantle is the core of the Earth, and it's made of metal. The inner core measures around 2440 km across and it composed of mostly iron and some nickel[ccxxix]. Around the inner core is liquid metal that extends for approximately 2000 km. This information is based on scientific measurements including seismic wave analysis.[ccxxx]

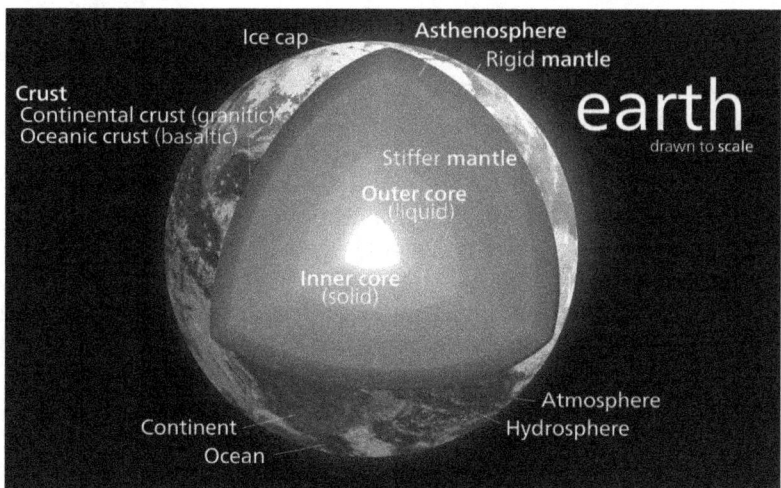

The Earth's Interior[ccxxxi]

Hell is described as having an eternal flame. If so, what is it that can provide an eternal supply of fuel to generate this heat energy without depletion? It is also not clear how a body can be continually burned. In the Quran, it is stated:

> "Those who have disbelieved - their wealth and their children will never benefit them anything with Allah. And those are the ones who are the fuel of Hellfire."
> [Quran 3: 10][ccxxxii]

There are some people with near death experiences that claim to have seen hell.[ccxxxiii] As discussed earlier, the veracity of these claims is questionable.

One might ask how one could deserve such a drastic penalty as eternal torment. One answer is that God cannot allow sinful man in His presence. This answer is contradictory to the claim that God is described as omnipresent. Of course, this would mean that God is present in hell, but this is often described as one definition of hell (the location where God is not).

In Christianity, another answer to how a God could send someone to hell for eternity is that we all deserve to go to hell for sinning. Another Christian doctrine is that all people sin because it is our nature to sin. Since all sin, all deserve hell because God made us the way we are (or that we are the descendants of Adam, who condemned mankind). One can say that God is God and He can do whatever He wants, but His actions reflects on His character. A God that would arbitrarily decide to make hell, and creatures (fallen angels including Satan) and humans that are destined for eternal punishment, is not be worthy of worship, since His nature could only be considered evil. An answer to this dilemma is that God made a way for man to avoid hell by accepting Jesus as their savior (Christianity). Similarly, a person could avoid hell by doing good as described in Islam. But some will not accept Jesus as their savior, and some may do evil outweighing their good in life. The penalty of an eternity in hell is a disproportionate penalty for any action that could be achieved during a lifetime.

Existence of Heaven

In the Bible, heaven is described as a place of eternal reward where God lives. There is limited information in the Torah and Bible describing heaven, so there are many differing thoughts on what heaven is like. Paradise, which is described in the Quran is described in more detail. Paradise is generally described as having seven layers with gates guarded by angels. Paradise includes beautiful maidens, precious stones, delicious food, and constantly flowing water[ccxxxiv]. In Hadith collections, paradise has as many as seventy-two virgins for male martyrs who are admitted.

According to Jewish tradition, the soul is lowered into Gehenna [place of spiritual punishment] for a maximum of 11 months after death to be cleansed of sins committed during life[ccxxxv]. Kaddish prayers are to be made by the loved ones of the deceased to protect the soul from harsh judgements[ccxxxvi].

What evidence do we have for the existence of heaven or paradise?

One may ask where is heaven? Several scriptures describe people being "caught up" to heaven, so generally heaven is considered above us but the location of heaven is not described and no one has discovered the location.

> And when he had said these things, as they were looking on, he was lifted up, and a cloud took him out of their sight. And while they were gazing into heaven as he went, behold, two women stood by them in white robes, and said, "Men of Galilee, why do you stand looking into heaven? This Jesus, who was taken up from you into heaven, will come in the same way as you saw him go into heaven."[ccxxxvii] Acts 1:9-11

There are those with near death experiences that claim to have been to heaven[ccxxxviii]. As discussed previously, the veracity of these claims is questionable.

One could ask how one could deserve such reward as an eternity in heaven. The general answer in Christianity is that man does not deserve such a reward and that it is through God's mercy that man is allowed into heaven by accepting the payment of Jesus' death for their sin. Some say that this destiny is predestined, while others claim it is the outcome of free will. If it is of free will, "Is it reasonable that one's eternal destiny be determined solely on acceptance of Jesus' payment for sin and/or adhering to the beliefs of Christianity? Does it seem somewhat capricious of God to make a system of punishment and reward based on belief an arbitrary rule that He determined and that not all people will have ever heard of?

Jesus as God

Some of the main denominations in Christianity claim that Jesus Christ was and is God. The following passages from the Bible can be used to support this view.

> In his defense Jesus said to them, "My Father is always at his work to this very day, and I too am working." For this reason, they tried all the more to kill him; not only was he breaking the Sabbath, but he was even calling God his own Father, making himself equal with God. John 5:17-18
>
> "You are not yet fifty years old," they said to him, "and you have seen Abraham!" Very truly I tell you," Jesus answered, "before Abraham was born, I am!" At this, they picked up stones to stone him, but Jesus hid himself, slipping away from the temple grounds. John 8:57-59

This sort of claim is not uncommon. Other religious leaders have claimed to be God or a god. Other religious leaders have claimed to be God or a god. Some examples include Moon Sun Myung (founder of the Unification Church), Jim Jones (founded the People's Temple), Shoko Asahara (founded the religious cult Aum Shrinkikyo), and Reverend M.J. Divine. Categorically the following also claimed to be gods: Pharaohs, Japanese, Chinese, and Roman emperors, Dalai Lamas, Inca emperors, and Nepalese kings.

What evidence is there that Jesus Christ was and is God?

Jesus was proposed to be born of God by Mary when she was a virgin. This claim would give Jesus a divine birth. This will be discussed more below. Jesus lived for around 33 years and then was killed by crucifixion. It is claimed that Jesus performed miracles during his life including changing water to wine, multiplying food, walking on water, miraculous healings, casting out demons, and resurrection of the dead. None of these miracles can be substantiated. Jesus was claimed to have been resurrected from the dead.

> The angel said to the women, "Do not be afraid, for I know that you are looking for Jesus, who was crucified. He is not here; he has risen, just as he said. Come and see the place where he lay. Then go quickly and tell his disciples: 'He has risen from the dead and is going ahead of you into Galilee. There you will see him.' Now I have told you."
> Matthew 28:5-7

Since Jesus was crucified and died on the cross, one may ask the question, how can God or at least a part of God die (note God is generally considered eternal)? In John 3:16, the Bible states:

> For God so loved the world that he gave his one and only Son, that whoever believes in him shall not perish but have eternal life.

This indicates that a separate part of God, the Son (Jesus Christ), was sent to die by another part of God (the Father). Some may claim that this dilemma is beyond human comprehension because God is beyond our comprehension.

Virgin Birth of Jesus

As, mentioned previously, it is claimed that Jesus was born of a virgin. All known humans are born through the union of human egg and sperm. This claim could only be explained supernaturally, since at the time *in vitro* fertilization was not known.

Group 2 – Hinduism, Buddhism, Jainism, and Sikhism

Let us move to a second group of related religions: Hinduism, Buddhism, Jainism, and Sikhism.

Hinduism

Some claims in Hinduism include:[ccxxxix]
- All beings are reincarnated - individual souls are immortal
- Truth is eternal
- Brahman is Truth and Reality

- The Vedas are the ultimate authority
- Everyone should strive to achieve dharma (moral law for conducting behavior)
- The goal of the individual soul is moksha (enlightenment)

Buddhism

Some claims in Buddhism include:[ccxl]
- Living beings are reincarnated in six possible realms (demigods, gods, men, animals, ghosts, and hell)
- Good or bad actions produce karma
- Life involves suffering
- All suffering is caused by craving
- Suffering can be overcome, and happiness attained (Nirvana)
- There is an eightfold path leading to overcoming suffering is:
    - Right understanding
    - Right thought
    - Right speech
    - Right action
    - Right livelihood
    - Right effort
    - Right mindfulness
    - Right concentration

Jainism

Some claims in Jainism include:[ccxli]
- All jivas or souls are reincarnated
- Liberation of the soul is impeded by accumulation of karmas[ccxlii]
- Karma can be freed from the soul by cultivating pure thoughts and actions
- By following the "Three Jewels" (right faith, right knowledge, and right conduct) one can achieve liberation of the soul[ccxliii]

Sikhism

Some claims in Sikhism include:[ccxliv]
- There is only one God without form of gender (see Mool Mantra below):

> There is one God
> His Name is Truth
> The All-pervading Creator,
> Without fear, without hatred
> Immortal, unborn, self-existent,
> By grace, the Enlightener.
> True in the beginning, true throughout the ages,
> True even now, Nanak, and forever shall be true.[ccxlv]

- All people are reincarnated until they have union with God

> By His writ some have pleasure, others pain,
> By His Grace some are saved,
> Others doomed to die relive and die again;
> His will encompasseth all, there be none beside,
> O Nanak, he who knows, hath no ego and no pride.
> (Japji 2)[ccxlvi]

- God can be experienced through love, worship, and contemplation
- God is inside everyone

> The Lord of man and beast is working in all;
> His presence is scattered everywhere; there is none else to be seen.
> One talks, another listens; God is in both.
> He is the Unity and Himself the Diversity. (Sukhmani XXII.1)[ccxlvii]

- Sikhs can gain unity with God through performing the three duties, which are:
    - Keeping God in mind at all times
    - Earning an honest living
    - Giving to charity and caring for others
- Sikhs are to avoid the five vices:
    - Lust
    - Rage
    - Greed
    - Attachment
    - Conceit

Reincarnation and Soul/Spirit

What evidence do we have of reincarnation of the soul or spirit?

While some people claim that they have been reincarnated, there is no reliable proof for these claims.[ccxlviii] It is unclear how credible these accounts of previous lives are, although several scientists have tried to examine these stories.[ccxlix]

As discussed previously, there is no reliable evidence for an eternal soul or spirit[ccl]. A soul has never been seen under an electron microscope or by any other means. Several individuals have tried to measure the theoretical loss of mass due to the departure of a soul from the body at death with no evidence of such[ccli]. Nothing appears to survive the human body after death. Scientific evidence supports that when we die our bodies decay and there is no other part of us. In support of this concept, we can see evidence that changes in hormones, neurotransmitters, and brain structure can change the personality of individuals. Thus, the individual is a function of the body, which is influenced by genetics and environmental conditions including experience.

Karma

What evidence do we have for karma?

According to Jainism karma is something that sticks to the soul and the soul needs to be freed from karma. As there is no evidence of a soul neither is there evidence of karma as a substance that sticks to the soul.

In Buddhism karma is the result of bad actions that influences the future life. Similarly, actions in life influence the next in Hinduism and actions in life influence the potential to have union with God in Sikhism. Thus, all these religions claim that actions in this life influence the next life after reincarnation. As discussed, there is no evidence for reincarnation. Thus, there is no evidence for karma to influence reincarnation.

Group 3 – Ancient Greece, Rome, and Egypt

For third group let us look at the claims associated with several polytheistic religions[cclii] such as that of ancient Greece, Rome, and Egypt.

Ancient Greek Religion

- Some claims of ancient Greek religion include:
- There are many gods, who reside on Mt. Olympus[ccliii].
- The gods have human bodies, marry, have children, and intervene in human affairs.
- The gods look favorably on prayer and sacrifices given to honor them.
- At death, the spirit leaves the body and goes to Hades[ccliv].
- If one lived a good life and was remembered by the living they can live in the pleasures of Elysium.
- If one was wicked, they go to the dark pits of Tartarus.
- If one is forgotten, they wander in the eternal bleakness of Hades.

Ancient Roman Religion

- There are many gods including the Greek gods.
- After death, the soul is separated from the corpse.
- After death, the soul is taken to the river Styx, which flows around the underworld ruled by Pluto.[cclv]
- After crossing the river Styx, one is judged.
- If one was a warrior or hero, they are sent to the Fields of Elysium.
- If one is an ordinary citizen, they are sent to the Plain of Asphodel.
- If one was judged to have committed a crime, they are to be tortured until the debt is paid.

Ancient Egyptian Religion

- There are many gods, which are involved in aspects of nature and human society.
- After death, the soul, which has several parts (ka, life force and ba, spiritual characteristics) [cclvi], goes the Hall of Truth[cclvii].
- After death, the deceased's heart is judged against the feather of truth and justice, where the actions of the deceased are judged.

Depiction of Heart Weighted Against Feather of Truth and Justice[cclviii]

- A heavy evil heart results in oblivion for eternity.
- A light righteous heart results in an afterlife with a transfigured spirit (akh).

What evidence do we have for many gods?

Many of these gods have bodies and are theoretically visible. In spite of this, there is no evidence of their existence.

What evidence do we have of a soul?

This has been discussed previously.

What evidence do we have of a judgement after death of the deeds done during life that influences the outcome of this afterlife?

This has also been discussed.

Discussion

Although we have only examined a few key claims of a few religions, we can see that the burden of proof has not been provided for these claims. Thus, the claims are merely that and to call them truth is inappropriate. There is a diversity of religions, which are incompatible. All religions can't all be true, but they can all be false.[cclix] Beliefs without evidence or proof are not reliable. While volumes could be written on the topic of the validity or lack of validity of religions, it is apparent that religions are the creation of people at various points in history. We have examined some of the reasons for the generation of these religions and the purpose that they serve.

Some religions promote various recommendations on how to conduct one's life. Some aspects of the moral codes of religions are beneficial for the preservation of the rights of mankind. Other moral codes generated by religions are arbitrary and merely serve to generate distinction of the believers from other religions or non-believers. For example, moral or behavioral codes related to dress, diet, and sexual behavior are often arbitrary and disparate among different religions. The incorporation of some appropriate and useful moral codes in a religion does not make the religion valuable considering that religions also include arbitrary and inappropriate moral codes. Society is not in need of arbitrary reasons for determining what is acceptable or beneficial behavior. Moral codes can be derived separate from religion[cclx].

It appears in America that there is an increasing number of people that do not identify with a religious group[cclxi]. Per Pew Research, the religious composition in the United States will continue show a drop in Christians and an increase in unaffiliated.

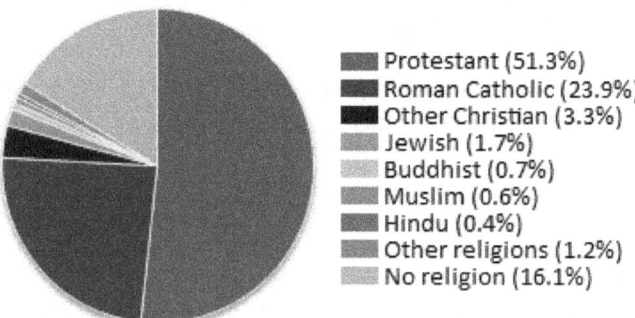

Religious Composition in the United States (2009)[cclxii]

According to Pew Research, many people who report "none" on religion state that they are scientists and do not believe in miracles. Other state that they do not believe in God because of common sense, logic, or a lack of evidence. Some state that they do not like the hierarchical nature of religious groups, think religion is too much like a business, or are concerned with clergy with sexual abuse scandals.

Churches are closing across the world and those who live their lives according to secular values and humanist principles are on the rise.

According to the Pew Research Center's latest estimates, there were over 1.1 billion non-religious people in the world in 2010, and that number is expected to increase to over 1.2 billion by the year 2020[cclxiii].

In Japan, about 70% of adults claimed to hold personal religious beliefs sixty years ago, but today, that figure is down to only about 20%. For the first time in British history, there are now more atheists and agnostics than believers in God[cclxiv]. Church attendance rates in the UK are less than 2% of the British attending church on any given Sunday. Nearly 70% of the Dutch are not affiliated with any religion. According to Pew's latest predictions, the growth of seculars will level off within a few decades, while Islam will continue to grow, becoming the world's largest religion by 2050.

Part 2 Implications of Religion

While some may agree that all religions are artificial, they may claim that religions serve a useful purpose and may have some positive influence on society[cclxv]. Let us examine whether this is correct.

Chapter 1 Community

Religions provide a belief system with associated behaviors that unify adherents and differentiate them from non-adherents. This provides a sense of community. These belief systems often define codes of behavior. The tendency of societies or groups within a society to alienate or repress different subcultures is recurrent in history. A person's religion can strongly influence their morality, worldview, self-image, attitudes towards others, and personal identity. Thus, religious differences can cause significant cultural and personal disunity.

Often religious leaders or figures are identified as father figures and are historically male. Freud regarded God as an illusion, based on the infantile need for a powerful father figure[cclxvi]. Those within the religion are sometimes referred to as brothers and the people that join religions are sometimes referred to as joining the family of God. These family related references may originate in some primitive religions and continued to give a sense of community. Such concepts enable people to perceive their actions for the good of their family, whereas normally people are not inclined to sacrifice for unrelated strangers.

People of a religion are often encouraged to meet together in a regular manner, which generates closer relationships. These regular meetings enable others to reinforce beliefs and indoctrinate newcomers to the religion. Often the children of believers are indoctrinated into their parent's religion at an early age and they are forced to attend services. For example, Hindu parents may be concerned that their children visit the temple regularly. The children are often encouraged to perform the rituals of the religion and adhere to the behavioral codes. Some parents home school children to keep them from the influences of the secular world and beliefs. Others send their children to special schools to learn the details of their parent's religion such as parochial schools for teaching the Talmud, Catholicism, or Islamic doctrine (Madrasa).

Alauddin Khalji's Madrasa in Delhi, India[cclxvii]

The act of dismissing the religion of the parents is generally not looked on favorably by the parents or the related community of believers. Dismissal of one's religion is often either not seriously considered or is done with significant penalty. In some cases, the rejection of one's family's religion can result in ostracism or being disowned by their family. In extreme cases this could be considered apostasy and result in death. The traditions of religion are often passed on as truth that must be upheld.

The act of participating in a religious community provides the potential for forming friendships and accomplishment of common goals. The process of praying for one another makes others aware of people's needs so that they can be acted upon. Some efforts conducted by religious groups can be beneficial to those in need such as providing food and rescue shelters, donations to those in need, and medical mission efforts. Some of these efforts are conducted for the good of those in need but also as an effort to convert unbelievers or to help brethren[cclxviii]. Some missions feed the hungry and nurse the sick. However, some do not do this for the good of humanity, but instead to convert people to Christianity[cclxix]. Often, religions target the poorest for conversions, not because they are the neediest, but because they can be bribed into changing their faith[cclxx]. Thus, while humanitarian efforts can be noble and positive, they are sometimes used as a means to propagate religion.

Missions

Many religious groups send out missionaries to promote their religion in other areas and start other likeminded religious communities. Conceptually, this is done to bring conversion for the benefit of the unbelievers. The purpose of Islamic missionary activity is to deliver the message revealed by God through the prophet Muhammad to the world. The Dharma Bhanaks[cclxxi] were missionaries that spread Buddhism throughout most the eastern world under the order of the Indian Emperor Ashoka the Great (c 250 BCE)[cclxxii]. Catholic missions were sent to the Americas to convert natives to Christianity and ease the transition of the natives into a colonial system[cclxxiii]. Establishment of missions were often followed by the implementation of encomienda systems.

If a person truly believed that their religion was true (the only truth) and cared for either the eternal destiny of others or the potential influence others actions would have on their reincarnation, it would be logical that they would want to share their religious beliefs with others. Considering the potential impact of not believing in Christianity or Islam (eternal hell), it would seem that a loving person would want to spend as much time and energy in helping others as possible. While this is the case for some believers and many missionaries, the majority of religious people do not act in this manner.[cclxxiv] There are a variety of reasons why people do not share their faith, including fear of rejection and that they are not truly sure that their religion is correct.[cclxxv]

Certain issues have brought criticism to missionary activity. This has included concerns that missionaries have a perceived lack of respect for other cultures. Potential destruction of social structure among the converts has also been a concern. The Akha people of South East Asia are an example of those who believe that missionaries are converting others for personal gain. The Akha people state that the missionaries are more interested in building churches than building clinics in villages that are unhealthy[cclxxvi]. A problem with granting poor nations money based on their religion is that nations are given monetary incentives to change their cultural traditions to receive funding.

In October 1975, just days after becoming an independent nation, East Timor was invaded by Indonesia; at this time, the population was about 72% Animist[cclxxvii]. The Catholic Church helped in the development of East Timor over the next 30 years. Under the oppression of the Indonesian occupation, the Catholic Church saw large conversion rates as it became the protection for the East Timorese. The church was a mechanism for non-violent protest against the occupation and a voice against the attacks taking place in the country. It can be argued that due to the presence of the Roman Catholic Church and its resources, many Animists converted as a means of survival.

Many countries are highly resistant to a religious change in their population. After the war in Iraq, evangelical Christians flooded the Iraq-Jordan border in attempts to convert citizens in the midst of relief efforts. In response, the resistance to many aid groups, religious or not, became violent and detrimental to the country. Violence against the established Christian minority living in Iraq erupted, so the attempts of religious conversion in administering foreign aid effectively led to the rejection of what religious pluralism may have existed in the strictly Islamic culture.

Discussion

Religions generate disagreement and differentiation of peoples, since there are many of different and opposing religions[cclxxviii]. While religious unity may generate a sense of community within the religion, it causes an attitude of disparity to people outside of their religion. This disparity enables an attitude of dislike or superiority of believers to non-believers. This attitude causes missionary tendencies and/or unequal treatment of people. While some actions generated by these communities may look like they are of good will, they are often self-serving efforts to convert others to their religion.

Chapter 2 Acceptable and Unacceptable Behaviors

Unacceptable behavior in some religions is sometimes termed sin or can be a different term in other religions such as immoral, unethical, or behavior generating negative karma. Sin (or unacceptable behavior) can be defined as an action that is opposed to God (or nature) or acting out of God's will. Sins can be of commission or omission. Individual religions define what is a sin or not (acceptable or not acceptable behaviors). Acceptable and not acceptable behaviors may change over time within a religion or may vary within sects of a religion. Some of these rules of behavior are logical, while many are not and are merely a method to make the believers unique (for example Buddhist monks and nuns shave their heads, wear robes, and wear a beaded bracelet called a mala[cclxxix]).

Some religions encourage their governments to make laws governing what they believe to be unacceptable or immoral behavior illegal. This has been the case in America due to the influence of fundamentalist Christian groups. This can be seen in the case of laws instituted for obscenity and sexual sins that were put in place during the second great awaking (early nineteenth century)[cclxxx]. Another example is Sharia law[cclxxxi], which is derived from the religious precepts of Islam, particularly the Quran and the Hadith. Attempts to impose Sharia on non-Muslims have caused intercommunal violence. Some Muslim-majority countries impose the death penalty or a prison sentence for apostasy from Islam or ban non-Muslims from proselytizing.

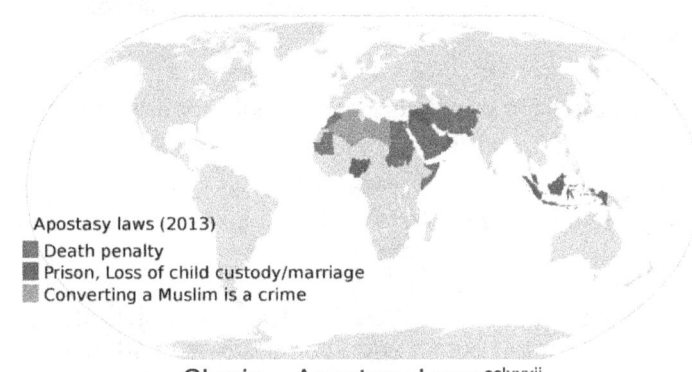

Apostasy laws (2013)
■ Death penalty
■ Prison, Loss of child custody/marriage
■ Converting a Muslim is a crime

Sharia – Apostasy Laws[cclxxxii]

Ethics in Buddhism

In Buddhism, there are codes of ethics or morality that include self-restraint or freedom from causing harm. Moral instructions are included in Buddhist scriptures or are handed down through tradition. One's past actions are said to affect the next life. The doing of good deeds is supposed to lead to a better condition in the rebirth.

There are five precepts in Buddha's teachings, which are[cclxxxiii]:
1. to abstain from taking life
2. to abstain from taking what is not given
3. to abstain from sensual misconduct
4. to abstain from false speech
5. to abstain from liquors, wines, and other intoxicants

Additional precepts listed in the Brahamajala Sutra[cclxxxiv]:
6. Not to broadcast the misdeeds or faults of the Buddhist assembly, nor encourage others to do so.
7. Not to praise oneself and speak ill of others or encourage others to do so.
8. Not to be stingy or encourage others to do so.
9. Not to harbor anger or encourage others to be angry.
10. Not to speak ill of the Buddha, the Dharma or the Sangha or encourage others to do so.

There are three additional precepts taken at specific religious days or retreats[cclxxxv]:
1. to abstain from food at improper times
2. to abstain from dancing, singing, instrumental music, and shows and from the use of jewelry, cosmetics, and beauty lotions
3. to abstain from the use of high and luxurious beds and seats.

The Brahmajala Sutra[cclxxxvi] includes a list of 10 major (including the five precepts listed above and five others) and 48 minor precepts, which prohibit the eating of meat, storing of weapons, teaching for profit, etc. Additionally, there are virtues that are promoted in Buddhism, which include good will, compassion, empathetic joy, and equanimity. Despite these precepts, some Buddhists including Japanese warrior monks have historically performed acts of violence. If the intention of killing is to protect others, the act of killing is sometimes seen as meritorious. While pacifism is a Buddhist ideal, Buddhist states and kingdoms have waged war throughout history.

Ethics in Hinduism

In Hinduism, the term "papa" is often used to describe actions that create negative karma by violating moral and ethical codes, which brings negative consequences[cclxxxvii]. Papa is considered a crime against the laws of God (Dharma), or moral order, and one's own self. The term papa is not the same as sin, since it is not an action against the will of God. This is because there is no consensus regarding the nature of God in Hinduism. Only the Vedanta school is theistic, whereas no anthropomorphic God exists in the other five schools, namely Sankhya, Nyaya, Yoga, Vaisesika, and Purvamimamsa.

Hindu ethics are mainly subjective or personal. Hindus try to eliminate mental impurities such as lust, wrath, and greed. The chief disciplines of subjective ethics are purity, self-control, detachment, truth, and non-violence. Social virtues include hospitality, courtesy, and duties to wife, children, and grandchildren.

The caste system defines the roles of people in this life. To conduct work that is outside of one's caste is considered shameful. The Bhagavad Gita describes the virtues of the four castes, and their duties[cclxxxviii].

- The qualities of a Brahmin are control of the mind and the senses, austerity, cleanliness, forbearance, uprightness, scholarship, insight, and faith. Brahmins are to possess a minimum of worldly assets, accept voluntary poverty, and are to be satisfied with simple living and high thinking. A Brahmin

is to be the leader of society and an adviser to the king and commoner. They are to be a custodian of the culture of the race, and to occupy a high position in society by virtue of their spirituality, and not by the power of arms or wealth.
- The qualities of a Kshatriya are heroism, high spirit, firmness, resourcefulness, dauntlessness in battle, generosity, and sovereignty.
- The duties of a Vaisya are agriculture, cattle rearing, and trade.
- The duty of a Sudra is physical labor.

The cow is greatly revered by Hindus and is regarded as sacred[cclxxxix]. Killing cows is banned in India and no Hindu would eat any beef product.

Sin in Islam

Muslims see sin as anything that is contrary to the commands of God (Allah). In Islam, only the prophets and angels are considered sinless. Islam teaches that sin is an act and not a state of being.

"The things that my Lord hath indeed forbidden are: shameful deeds, whether open or secret; sins and trespasses against truth or reason; assigning of partners to Allah, for which He hath given no authority; and saying things about Allah of which ye have no knowledge." Quran 7:33

Listed below are some of the serious sins in Islam[ccxc]:
- Worshipping others with Allah

    "Verily, whosoever sets up partners in worship with Allah, then Allah has forbidden Paradise for him, and the Fire will be his abode. And for the Zalimoon (polytheists and wrongdoers) there are no helpers" Quran 5:72

- Witchcraft
- Killing a soul whom Allah has forbidden to be killed

- Usury
- Taking an orphan's wealth
- Fleeing from Jihad
- Slandering chaste, innocent believing women

    "And those who accuse chaste women, and produce not four witnesses, flog them with eighty stripes" Quran 24:4

- Disrespect for parents
- To swear falsely by the name of Allah
- Fornication or adultery
- Homosexuality
- To withhold zakat (share of money and like required by Islamic law)
- To drink or eat blood

Sin in Judaism

According to Judaism, the minimal moral duties of all men are to observe the Laws of Noah.

The seven Laws of Noah[ccxci] are:
1. Do not deny God
2. Do not blaspheme God
3. Do not murder
4. Do not engage in incestuous, adulterous or homosexual relationships.
5. Do not steal
6. Do not eat of a live animal
7. Establish courts/legal systems to ensure law obedience

Mainstream Judaism regards the violation of any of the 613 commandments (Mitzvot)[ccxcii] of the Mosaic law for Jews as sin. These commandments include instruction on such things as circumcision, reciting grace after meals, not to afflict an orphan or widow, how to treat strangers, marriage and divorce, forbidden sexual relations, dietary laws, business practices, judicial procedures, idolatry, clothing, tithes and taxes, sacrifices and offerings, and conduct of war.

Let us now discuss some specific types behaviors and examine what is acceptable or not acceptable according to different religions.

Sexual Behavior

Several religions permit polygamy (although polygamy is not legal in many countries except in some parts of Africa, the Middle East, and a few countries in southeastern Asia)[ccxciii].

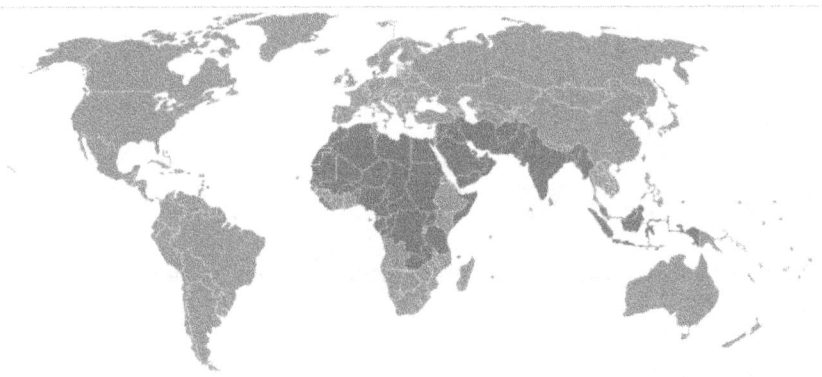

Countries Where Polygamy is Legal[ccxciv]

Many of the patriarchs of Judaism were polygamists. Some sects of the Mormon Church continue today to practice polygamy. In the Quran polygamy is allowed.

The Oneida Community, founded by John Humphrey Noyes in 1848 in Oneida, New York believed in a system of free love, where any member was free to have sex with any other who consented. Possessiveness and exclusive relationships were frowned upon[ccxcv]. Raising children was a communal responsibility. Women over the age of forty were to act as sexual mentors to adolescent boys, as these relationships had minimal chance of conceiving.

John Humphrey Noyes, (1811-1886). He founded the Oneida Community in 1848[ccxcvi]

Buddhist monks and nuns of most traditions are expected to take vows of celibacy as in the case of Catholic priests and nuns. Likewise, Jain monks and nuns are to abstain from sex and sensual pleasures. The requirement of celibacy has generated many instances of non-compliance for priests, monks, and nuns. The Shakers, founded in 18th century England, practiced celibacy and communal lifestyle[ccxcvii]. Procreation was forbidden after they joined the Shaker society.

Life of the Diligent Shaker, Shaker Historical Society[ccxcviii]

Many religions consider homosexual behavior as a sin including most of Judaism, Christianity, and Islam. Christian groups in the United States have been responsible for much of the persecution of gays and lesbians[ccxcix]. This persecution has involved promoting laws against homosexuality, discharge from the military, and loss of employment. Passages from the Mosaic Covenant and its broader Old Testament context have been interpreted to mean that anyone engaging in homosexual practices should be punished with death.

> Leviticus 20:13[ccc]
> If a man has sexual relations with a man as one does with a woman, both of them have done what is detestable. They are to be put to death; their blood will be on their own heads.

All major Islamic schools disapprove of homosexuality[ccci]. Homosexual intercourse is illegal under Sharia law, though the prescribed penalties differ from one school of jurisprudence to another.[cccii] For example, some Muslim-majority countries impose the death penalty for acts perceived as sodomy and homosexual activities: Iran, Saudi Arabia, and in other Muslim-majority countries such as Egypt, Iraq, and the Indonesian province of Aceh, same-sex sexual acts are illegal, and Lesbian Gay Bisexual Trans-sexual people regularly face violence and discrimination. The Mormons teach that those who experience same-sex attraction should exercise self-control and reliance on the atonement of Jesus Christ to refrain from acting on such feelings. Although homosexuals are a minority, homosexuals are approximately 10% of the general population per the Kinsey Reports,[ccciii] although it may be higher than that per a 2002 Gallup poll of Americans[companion ccciv].

Catholics, protestants, and Mormons have condemned masturbation as a sin[cccv]. Sunni Islam has varying opinions on masturbation but considers it a bad habit. Although homosexuality and masturbation do not lead to procreation, these forms of behavior are seen in nature. Based on the biblical story of Onan, traditional Judaism condemns male masturbation.

> But Onan knew that the child would not be his; so whenever he slept with his brother's wife, he spilled his semen on the ground to keep from providing offspring for his brother. What he did was wicked in the Lord's sight; so the Lord put him to death also. Genesis 38:9-10

Different schools of Buddhism have differing interpretations of what constitutes sexual misconduct. In Taoism, some practitioners say that males should not practice martial arts for at least 48 hours after masturbation while others prescribe up to six months, because the loss of origin qi does not allow new qi to be created for this kind of time. Some Taoists discourage female masturbation. Women were encouraged to practice massaging techniques upon themselves but were also instructed to avoid thinking sexual thoughts if experiencing a feeling of pleasure. Otherwise, the woman's "labia will open wide and the sexual secretions will flow."[cccvi] If this happened, the woman would lose part of her life force, could bring illness, and have a shortened life.

The circumcision of males, which is practiced in Judaism and Islam is a method of differentiating those of that believers from non-believers. Although the practice predates both religions, it was adopted as a command in the Hebrew Bible in Genesis chapter 17. There are debates as to potential positive (lower HIV infection rate) and negative effects (decreased sensitivity and protective tissue) of this procedure, but ultimately this is an elective procedure.

Abortion is considered as an evil act by some Buddhists because of their concept of rebirth being present at conception. Hinduism strongly condemns abortion, although abortions in India are legal up to twelve weeks in gestation. Sex determination cannot generally be determined until later. Although illegal, some clinics in India offer a both an ultrasound test and an abortion if the fetus is female (considered a burden to the family considering the need for a dowry). Most all Christian denominations including the Catholic and Eastern Orthodox Churches are considered pro-life, while a minority may be considered pro-choice. Orthodox Jews sanction abortion only if needed to safeguard the life of the pregnant woman, whereas Reformed, Reconstructionist, and Conservative Jews advocate the right to a safe abortion. Most Muslims "agree that the termination of a pregnancy after 120 days, the point at which, in Islam, a fetus is thought to become a living soul, is not permissible."[cccvii] Abortion and permanent sterilization are forbidden to those of the Baha'i faith unless there is a medical reason for it[cccviii]. Rastafrians are opposed to abortion and contraception[cccix]. The Unitarian Universalist Church and the Wiccans support abortion rights.

Dress Codes

Dress codes are less about clothing than about differentiation of believers from non-believers by religious authorities who enforce their groups' ideologies. Religious dress codes express group identity and simultaneously function to show visual conformism. Nudism is considered a sin in most religions, although recreational nudism is permissible by some Christian naturists. Also, monks in the Digambara sect of Jainism do not wear clothes while the Svetambara sect of Jainism wear white clothes[cccx]. Monks of the Naga sect of Hinduism often only wear a loincloth[cccxi]. Some Wiccan groups perform some of their rituals skyclad[cccxii] (nude).

Acharya Vidyasagar, a prominent Digambara monk of modern India[cccxiii]

Christian baptisms were originally conducted without clothing until around 700 CE. The ability to use skins from other animals or to make clothes from other sources has the advantage of providing protection and warmth but the mandate that some portions of the body be covered is culturally or religiously defined. Examples include the Islamic hijab (head covering), burqa (body cover with veil), Jewish Yamaka or kippah[cccxiv].

Detail of the head and upper torso portions of a silk burqa (left)[cccxv]
Aron Marcus (1800-1882) wearing his kippah (right)[cccxvi]

For Hasidic Jewish women, wigs are worn to cover their natural hair. Also, Hasidic Jewish men do not shave the sides of their faces. Hindus consider footwear to be impure. Hindus are not to wear shoes or sandals inside the temple or in their homes. Cutting hair is forbidden in Sikhism for those who have taken the Amrit[cccxvii] initiation ceremony. Sikhs are required to wear the five Ks, which are the Kesh (uncut hair), Kangha (a wooden comb for the hair), Kara (an iron or steel bracelet), Kachera (cotton undergarment), and Kirpan (an iron dagger or steel sword)[cccxviii].

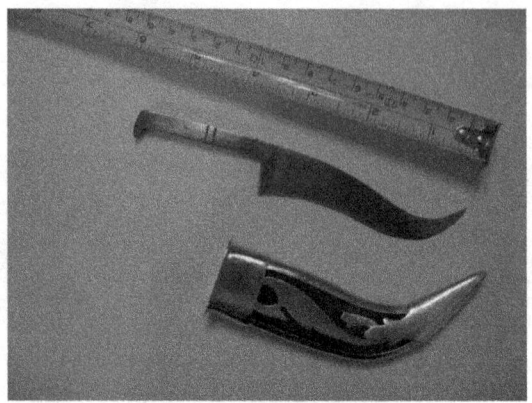
Kirpan with ruler[cccxix]

Rastafarians[cccxx] are forbidden to cut their hair. Instead, they twist it into dreadlocks.

Gender Inequality

There is a spectrum of attitudes toward gender roles in the various religions and gender roles in some religions have changed over time. Some Jews recite a morning prayer that states "Blessed are you O God, King of the Universe, who has not made me a woman"[cccxxi]. Although this sounds disparaging to women, some explain that this does not mean that women are not equal[cccxxii]. In general, although there is a larger proportion of women than men in Christian churches, there are few women in leadership roles in most churches except in roles over other women or children. In 1 Timothy 2:12, Paul states that women should not teach or exercise authority over men. In Genesis 2, man is created first, followed by woman. The first woman (Eve) is created from the rib of the first man (Adam), as a companion and helper. This version is normally cited by Jewish authorities in support of patriarchy, and likewise by Christians. A similar story appears in the Quran[cccxxiii]. Abortions in India (largely a Hindu nation) are almost all of females and not males. Women are considered as a financial burden because of the dowry that is to be provided at their marriage. Although not practiced currently, Sati was a funeral custom where the widow commits suicide by putting herself on the husband's funeral pyre or commits suicide by another means.

An 18th-century painting depicting sati[cccxxiv]

A woman in Hinduism is to obey and seek protection from her parents. Then she is to be protected by her husband and widows are to be protected by their sons.

Slavery

The teachings of Judaism, Christianity, and Islam, which are based on their scriptures are not anti-slavery and many adherents to these religions have been involved in the sale and ownership of slaves. The Muslim Arabs and Christian Europeans enslaved large populations from Africa.

13th-century slave market in Yemen[cccxxv]

The slave trade generated substantial wealth for those involved. Many Africans died during the capture, transport, and use of the slaves. These humans were treated as property by these religious adherents. The Bible does not consider owning slaves as a sin. This is interesting, as slavery is no longer legal anywhere in the world. In 1981 Mauritania became the last country in the world to abolish slavery[cccxxvi].

Slavery has not been limited to only these groups. Slavery was part of Greek and Roman life (not precluded by Greek and Roman religions). One famous slave uprising of note was that of Spartacus against the Roman rule. Slaves were commonly the victims of loss in battle. The Vikings took slaves from raids in Europe. Spain and Portugal saw constant warfare between Muslims and Christians (enslaving those captured in battle). Similarly, many Christians were enslaved by the Muslims during the Byzantine-Ottoman wars. While black slavery was never widespread among Mormons, there were several prominent slave owners in the leadership of the Latter Day Saints Church. Brigham Young also encouraged members to participate in the Indian slave trade. While visiting the members in Parowan, he encouraged them to "buy up the Lamanite [American Indian] children as fast as they could".

A statue of Chief Walkara, a Mormon slave trader[cccxxxvii]

Dietary

Various religions have developed rules regarding what foods are not to be eaten as part of their moral laws. The Old Testament defines foods that are sinful to eat. The Jews have restrictions on how meat is slaughtered, which animals, birds, and seafood may be eaten, the part of the animal that can be eaten, and allowable combinations of foods. Muslims are only to eat meat that is slaughtered according to halal. Pork is non-halal. Also, blood and alcoholic beverages are considered non-halal, which involves killing through a cut to the jugular vein, carotid artery, and trachea[cccxxxviii].

Hinduism indicates that the cow is sacred and not to be eaten. Mormonism prohibits the consumption of alcohol and caffeine. Some Buddhists believe that vegetarianism is consistent with the precept of not taking life; while most Buddhists eat meat. Evidently, some Buddhist vegetarians do not consider plants as life or perhaps they do not kill the plants as part of the consumption. Jains are strict vegetarians[cccxxix]. Additionally, Hindu women are not to drink alcohol or smoke in public. Seventh-day Adventists practice a vegetarian diet and coffee, tea, and alcoholic beverages are not to be consumed[cccxxx]. Rastafarians follow strict dietary laws and abstain from alcohol. Their communal meetings are typified by the smoking of cannabis, which is regarded as a sacrament. Rastas eat food that is natural or pure from the earth. Rastas diet is called Ital, which includes a diet that is devoid of salt, oil, and meat[cccxxxi]. Some Christian sects do not allow consumption of alcohol and Roman Catholics have restrictions of eating meat on certain days. Fasting is practiced in Roman Catholicism, Mormonism, Judaism, Islam, and Hinduism.

Among the Gimi of Papua New Guinea cannibalism is rooted in ancient mythology where the "mother" figure is depicted as a punishing deity. The Gimi attribute such problems as male impotence, lack of milk in new mothers, and female infertility to the "mother" robbing vital energy from the dead, thus leaving less for the living. Gimi cannibalism is primarily a ritual whereby women eat the bodies of their own children, husbands, and parents as a way to counteract the life-draining powers of the mother deity. The Aghori (Hindu Sect) frequently consume meat and routinely include alcohol in their daily rituals. It is their belief that eating the dead will give them a direct pathway to god, avoiding reincarnation[cccxxxii].

Aghori: Cannibal Sect of Hindu Monks[cccxxxiii]

Medical Care

While most religions take advantage of the advances in medical care that have been developed by scientists, inventors, and healthcare workers, there are some groups that refuse treatment. Jehovah Witnesses forbid their followers from receiving blood transfusions. There are also some religious groups such as Christian Scientists that believe prayer is more powerful than medical care and have rejected medical care for themselves or their children. Certain religions and belief systems promote alternative perspectives toward vaccination. Religious objections to vaccines are based generally on the using human tissue cells to create vaccines, and beliefs that the body is sacred, should not receive certain chemicals or blood or tissues from animals, and should be healed by God or natural means[cccxxxiv]. The result of some of these beliefs has led to the suffering and death of adherents or their children. The Church of Scientology has strong opposition to medical specialties such as psychiatry and psychology. There have been several cases in which Scientologists have been taken out of or not received psychiatric care, which ultimately resulted in deaths (see cases of Lisa McPherson and Jeremy Perkins)[cccxxxv].

Scientologists holding an anti-psychiatry demonstration[cccxxxvi]

Followers of Shintoism are generally opposed to organ transplantation. They consider interfering with a corpse as bad luck and that the body is impure after death. This leads Shinto followers to oppose organ transplantation and would refuse receiving an organ from someone who has died[cccxxxvii].

Discussion

Since believers of specific religions consider that they have truth in their religion, they believe that they have knowledge of how they and others should live their lives. These rules of behavior can encompass many aspects of life including diet, dress, sexual behavior, and treatment of others. Some of these rules of behavior are arbitrary and are of little consequences (as in some types of diet and dress). Other rules of behavior can have a negative impact on the adherents such as refusal of medical care or preferential treatment based on sex. There are other rules of behavior that are considered as universally beneficial for society such as abstaining from murder and false testimony. Those in authority may generate rules of behavior with punishment for those that do not behave in agreement with the rules. These punishments can vary from shunning to death depending on the importance of the rule (based on the religion's definition or their ability to influence the ruling authority). While punishment may be appropriate for some uncivil behaviors, it may be best left to government authorities to address these issues.

Chapter 3 Positive Aspects of Religion

There are some aspects of religion that are positive such as in the case of providing a sense of identity and community. We have discussed these areas earlier in the book. Some might consider a sense of purpose as another potential positive aspect of religion but as discussed previously religions do not provide the burden of evidence to substantiate their claim of an afterlife (or reincarnation). Thus, this sense of purpose is likely misplaced. Although we have already briefly touched on some of the positive aspects of religion in promoting moral behavior and in providing service to others (good deeds), we will look at these two aspects a bit closer.

Promotion of Moral Behavior

First, we must determine what we mean by moral behavior. While some believe that certain acts are moral, others would not agree. So, how do we determine what is moral and what is morality? According to Merriam-Webster the term moral is defined as "of or relating to principles of right and wrong in behavior."[cccxxxviii] Thus, we must determine what is right or wrong in behavior. We might ask, "Who defines right and wrong?"

According to many religions, right and wrong are defined by a deity or by laws defined by a deity. If there is no actual deity, this means that right and wrong are defined by people who are authorities in the various religions. If we leave religion out of how we define right and wrong, then right and wrong may be defined by political or legal authorities. While political and legal authorities can be flawed in developing codes of moral behavior, there is the potential for using rationale, logical, and appropriate moral codes that are based on promoting the welfare for those under these authorities.

A motivation for developing rules and laws of behavior is to promote the welfare of the group. For example, a rule of not stealing another's property is likely to benefit most people in society. Considering the actions of a thief as immoral and potentially worthy of punishment promotes a more peaceful existence. A rule of not murdering others, promotes safety for those in a group, which may enable productivity and increased population. Many laws of morality have positive benefits for the group or society. Thus, it is not necessary for a religion to define or promote morality. Freud stated that religion, which was needed to help restrain violent impulses earlier in the development of civilization, can be set aside in favor of reason and science[cccxxxix].

There are a number of religions that promote moral behavior and encourage positive self-traits. Shintoism promotes harmony of mankind and nature. As discussed earlier, Buddhism encourages abstaining from taking life, taking what is not given, sensual misconduct, and false speech. Judaism includes prohibitions against murder and stealing. Jainism promotes non-violence, truth, not stealing, and chastity. Ironically, many religions that promote morality permit or encourage activities that would normally be considered as immoral or sometimes illegal (see discussion of persecution and religious wars).

Good Deeds

Let us look a bit closer at the fact that some religions encourage helping others and provide humanitarian welfare. Some Christian organizations include[cccxl]:
- Compassion International (focused on releasing children from economic, physical, and spiritual poverty),
- Food for the Hungry (providing food, shelter, and clothing for the needy),
- World Vision (mission of helping the poor, provide emergency relief, economic development, promote justice and spread awareness of countries in need), and
- Samaritan's Purse (helping the poor, assisting people with physical needs as well as engaging in missionary work) provide humanitarian welfare.

Tzu Chi is the world' largest Buddhist charity[cccxli]. Tzu Chi provides food and medical care to illegal immigrants in the US, distributes emergency supplies, and food in case of disasters.

Sewa International is a Hindu organization that provides disaster rescue, relief, and rehabilitation[cccxlii].

These and many other organizations are faith-based organizations that provide benefit to those in need. The question is whether religion encourages humanitarian efforts that would otherwise not exist and whether the motivation for these efforts is in part coupled with a desire to evangelize the beneficiaries.

Below is a list of some non-religious based humanitarian organizations:
- Amnesty International (bringing refugee families together)[cccxliii]
- UNICEF (providing food for children)[cccxliv]
- Doctors Without Borders (responding to medical emergencies)[cccxlv]
- WaterAid (improving access to safe water, sanitation and hygiene)[cccxlvi]

It can be seen that religion is not necessary for the development and execution of humanitarian efforts. The next question is whether the motivation of religious humanitarian efforts is in part coupled to a desire to evangelize the beneficiaries.

Research from the University of California, Berkeley (published in the online issue of the Journal Social Psychological and Personality Science)[cccxlvii] suggests that highly religious people are less motivated by compassion when helping a stranger than are atheists, agnostics, and less religious people. Social scientists found that compassion drove fewer religious people to be more generous. For highly religious people compassion was largely unrelated to how generous they were. Thus, we might ask what is the motivation of highly religious people to help others. Some religions teach that helping others is a dictum of their religion. Thus, in some cases the motivation for helping others may be out of obligation.

A few other motivations of the highly religious could be to obtain good karma for themselves or to do good deeds to obtain reward in heaven. As proposed earlier, some of these humanitarian efforts of religious organizations may also serve in part as a mechanism to reach those who are of other religions that are in a vulnerable state, who can be evangelized. This is evidenced in the mission statements of some of these organizations in that they are also "engaging in missionary work" or addressing "spiritual poverty."

Discussion

Some appropriate and largely universal morals are promoted by religions. These moral actions are of general benefit to society. There is also good done in the name of religion and by those involved in religion. This demonstrates that not all actions of religions are detrimental to society. Moral and ethical behavior, and humanitarian efforts are not dependent on religion. Religions disagree on what is moral and find methods to enable immoral behavior in the name of their religions (see Chapters on Persecution and Religious Wars). The good deeds of the highly religious may be tainted by ulterior motives other than compassion for those in need.

Chapter 4 Persecution

Those who do not adhere to a specific religion or specific doctrines within a religion are sometimes persecuted by believers in other or similar religions[cccxlviii]. Also, people of various religions are sometimes persecuted by those that see the believers in certain religions as agents of corruption of their customs and societal values.

Persecution may include confiscation or destruction of property, hate, arrest, imprisonment, beatings, torture, and execution.[cccxlix] Non-compliant individuals may be forced to live as second class citizens, ostracized, or killed. Usually the group that is in majority persecutes those with minority beliefs. Persecution of those of different opinions, races, and cultures is not uncommon in history. Differences in religious beliefs are another excuse for persecution.

Persecution of Hindus

Mahmud Ghazni invaded India about 1000 AD, which began Muslim invasions of the Indian subcontinent[cccl]. The Muslim conquest of the Indian subcontinent led to widespread carnage because Muslims regarded the Hindus as infidels and therefore slaughtered and converted millions of Hindus. The holocaust of Hindus in India continued for about 800 years.

Records indicate that tens of millions of Hindus, Sikhs, Buddhists, and Jainists were killed[cccli]. There were mass rapes of women, abduction of Hindu women and children to slave markets, and destruction of temples and libraries. Even those Hindus who converted to Islam were not immune from persecution through the Muslim Caste System in India. Hindus who converted to Islam were regarded as the low-born caste and subjected to severe discrimination by the Ashraf (noble) castes who claimed foreign ancestry and were considered conquerors[ccclii].

Persecution of Buddhists

Persecution of Buddhists has been a widespread phenomenon throughout the history of Buddhism lasting to this day. Persecutions are recorded as early as the third century AD by the Zoroastrian Sassanid Empire[cccliii]. Some of the persecutions included the following:

Emperor Wuzong Tang (814-846) was a zealous Taoist who considered other religions as harmful to China. He persecuted Buddhists, Zoroastrians, and Manichaeists[cccliv] (a religion founded by the Iranian prophet Mani in 216 CE, which describes a struggle between good and evil), and Nestorian Christians. Wuzong saw Buddhism as a foreign religion that was harmful to Chinese society. Anti-Buddhist sentiments in China between the fifth and tenth century led to the Four Buddhist Persecutions in China of which the Great Anti-Buddhist Persecution of 845[ccclv] was probably the most severe. Thousands of temples were destroyed, and metal objects melted down for hard currency. Many monks and nuns were forced to return to lay life, so they could contribute to the general tax base.

Mahmud of Ghazni, Muslim and Sultan of the Ghaznavid Empire in 997-1030, destroyed the most delicately carved and expressive images of the Buddha and treasures of the Buddha art. He looted and burned down monasteries, and killed Buddhist scholars, making Buddhist monks take refuge in Tibet.

The Nalanda University, a Buddhist center of learning, was raided by Turkic Muslim invaders under Bakhtiyar Khalji, a general of the Turkish commander Qutb-ud-din Aybak, in 1193. He committed executions, harassed, and tortured monks, killing 15,000 scholars and 200 faculty of the University.

In the twentieth century Buddhists were persecuted by Asian communist states and parties, Imperial Japan, and by the Nationalist Party of China. The Chinese Communists invaded Tibet and occupied the region in 1950. They suppressed the monastic orders that had been for many centuries in Tibet and more than 1.2 million Tibetans were killed. In 1959, the Tibetans made a revolt against the Chinese, only to fail and face an even harsher policy designed to completely eradicate Tibetan Buddhism. Temples and monasteries were looted and razed, Buddhist treasures, statues and holy items were taken to China, scriptures were burnt, and monks and nuns were imprisoned or killed. About 100,000 refugees escaped to India and other surrounding countries. The Dalai Lama fled to India and establish a government-in-exile there, as he and his followers were denounced to be enemies of the state. During the 1966-1976 Cultural Revolution, the more than 6,200 monasteries in Tibet were destroyed.[ccclvi]

Persecution of Judaism

Throughout Jewish history, persecutions have been committed by the Seleucids, ancient Greeks, ancient Romans, Christians (Catholics, Orthodox, and Protestant), Muslims, Communists, Nazis, etc. During history some Christians have rationalized persecution the Jews based on the Jews being responsible for killing of Jesus. Also, the Jews were in some cases considered scapegoats for the Black Death epidemics in Europe. Some of the most important events include:

- 1066 Granada massacre – Muslim massacre of Jews in Granada
- Persecution of Jews in the First Crusade (1096) including the Rhineland massacres
- Second crusade – Jews in France were massacred
- Alhambra Decree after the Reconquista expelling Jews from Castile and Aragon and the creation of the Spanish Inquisition
- Publication of "On the Jews and Their Lies" by Martin Luther, which initiated the protestant antisemitism and strengthened German antisemitism
- Russian pogroms or riots[ccclvii]
- The Holocaust (1941-1945), culminating in the killing of approximately 6 million Jews during which Jews were often forced into ghettos and then transported to concentration camps

Polish Jews Captured by Germans during the Warsaw Ghetto Uprising, May 1943[ccclviii]

Persecution of Christians

The persecution of Christians can be seen historically and in the current century. From the beginning of the religion as a movement within Judaism, Christians were persecuted for their faith by both the Jews and the Roman Empire.

The Stoning of Stephen Saint-Etienne-du-Mont[ccclix]

The first Christian martyr is considered to be Stephen, who was accused of blasphemy by the Jews and then was stoned to death. Many of the apostles of Christ were martyred including Peter, who was crucified upside-down according to legend. Some Christians were executed in the Roman colosseum because of their potential threat to Roman society including Saint Ignatius. This continued from the first century until the early fourth, when the religion was legalized by the Edict of Milan, eventually becoming the State church of the Roman Empire.

In 1758 the king of Korea, Yeongjo of Joseon outlawed Catholicism as an "evil practice." Joseon royalty saw the new religion as a subversive influence and persecuted its earliest followers in Korea, culminating in the Catholic Persecution of 1866, in which 8,000 Catholics across the country were killed, including nine French missionary priests.

Sinhalese Buddhist nationalists concerns with the country's Buddhist hegemony being challenged by Christian proselytism led to Buddhist monks and organizations to demonize Christian organizations.[ccclx] Sinhalese Buddhist nationalists, who oppose attempts to convert Buddhists to another religion, support or conduct anti-Christian violence. The number of attacks against Christian churches rose from 14 in 2000 to over 100 in 2003. Dozens of these acts were confirmed by U.S. diplomatic observers. This anti-Christian violence was led by extremist Buddhist clergy and has included acts of "beatings, arson, acts of sacrilege, death threats, violent disruption of worship, stoning, abuse, unlawful restraint, and even interference with funerals."

Christians are still persecuted in countries such as North Korea, Afghanistan, Somalia, Sudan, Pakistan, Libya, Iraq, Yemen, and Iran.[ccclxi] Similarly, Christians have persecuted believers of other religions such as Judaism, Islam, and other Christians of differing denominations.

Persecution of Mormons

In 1844, a rift developed between Joseph Smith, the founder of the Latter-Day Saint movement, and a half dozen of his closest associates. Believing the dissidents were plotting against his life, Smith excommunicated them. These dissidents formed a competing church and they procured indictments against Smith for perjury and polygamy. Smith and his brother Hyrum were to stand trial for inciting a riot and treason but were killed by an armed mob[ccclxii]. Below is an illustration of the murder of Joseph Smith and his brother Hyrum Smith, which are considered as religious martyrs by the members of the Latter-Day Saint movement (Mormons).

Anti-Mormonism – Killing of Joseph Smith, Founder of the Latter-Day Saint Movement[ccclxiii]

Persecution of the Mormon Church from the US government existed from 1858-1896, largely due to the church's practice of polygamy. In 1882, the Edmunds Act, which outlawed cohabitation with more than one woman, was passed. To enforce this, U.S. President Chester A. Arthur sent the Utah Commission. All Mormons who practiced polygamy were stripped of the right to vote and forbidden to hold public office. Many of them were also jailed. The Latter-Day Saints initially labeled such publications "anti-Christian."

Inquisition

The Inquisition was a group of institutions within the government system of the Catholic Church whose aim was to combat heresy[ccclxiv]. The inquisition started in 12th-century France to combat the religious sectarianism of the Cathars and the Waldensians. Cathars believed in a modified version of Catholicism with dualism and reincarnation[ccclxv]. Waldensians deviated from the Catholic Church in that they rejected some of the seven sacraments[ccclxvi]. During the Late Middle Ages and early Renaissance, the concept and scope of the Inquisition significantly expanded in response to the Protestant Reformation and the Catholic Counter-Reformation. It expanded to other European countries, resulting in the Spanish Inquisition and Portuguese Inquisition.

The Spanish and Portuguese operated inquisitorial courts throughout their empires in Africa, Asia, and the Americas (resulting in the Peruvian Inquisition and Mexican Inquisition). The Spanish and Portuguese inquisitions focused particularly on the issue of Jewish and Muslim converts to Catholicism, partly because these minority groups were more numerous in Spain and Portugal than in many other parts of Europe, and because they were often considered suspect due to the assumption that they had secretly reverted to their previous religions. The inquisitions in some cases used torture to obtain confession from the suspected heretics. In many cases those convicted of heresy were burned at the stake.

Though not subject to the Inquisition, Jews who refused to convert or leave Spain were called heretics and could be burned to death on a stake[ccclxvii]

During the Spanish inquisition, there were cases in which the level of evidence required for conviction was highly suspect. The use of circumstantial evidence and hidden witnesses lead to probable cases in which there were false convictions. Regardless of the accuracy of the charges of heresy, it is noteworthy that death sentences for differences in beliefs within the Catholic church is a reflection on the ruthlessness of some believers.

Witch Trials

Belief in witchcraft and persecutions directed at it were widespread in pre-Christian Europe. This was reflected in Germanic law. Throughout the medieval era mainstream Christian teaching denied the existence of witches and witchcraft, condemning it as pagan superstition. This is interesting, since witchcraft is mentioned in the Bible in multiple passages including:

> "He sacrificed his children in the fire in the Valley of Ben Hinnom, practiced divination and witchcraft, sought omens, and consulted mediums and spiritists. He did much evil in the eyes of the LORD, arousing his anger." II Chronicles 33:6

The denunciation and persecution of supposed sorceresses that characterized the witch hunts of a later age were not generally found in the first thirteen hundred years of the Christian era.

Although the persecution of alleged witches took place in the Christian Europe during the medieval period, it reached its peak during the religious wars of the 16th and 17th centuries.[ccclxviii] In that period, laws in many Catholic and Protestant countries enforced the belief that witchcraft was the work of the devil. Historians estimate that between 40,000 and 60,000 people were executed for witchcraft in Europe, and the American colonies from the 15th to the early 18th centuries, although it is possible the number is larger[ccclxix]. One estimate is between 30,000 and 100,000 witches were killed in Old Europe. Some countries killed less than ten (Portugal and Ireland), while others (Germany, Switzerland and France) killed tens of thousands. In most of these countries, they tended to hang the victims, but in Denmark and Norway the preference was to burn them[ccclxx].

Approximately 75 percent of the victims were women. Several celebrated witch trials in Denmark resulted in the executions of hundreds of people. Historians estimate that around 250 alleged witches were executed in the Danish district of Jutland during the 1600s. The Danish witch trial and the alleged magical attack on his bride spurred King James to start the first of five "great witch hunts" in Scotland. In America, there were a series of witch trials in Salem Massachusetts in 1692-1693.[ccclxxi] The trials resulted in the executions of twenty people, while five others died in prison. This is an example of a dangerous effect of errant belief propagated by religious belief and fervor.

1876 illustration of the courtroom of Salem witch trial[ccclxxii]

Sikh Protests

Jarnail Singh Bhindranwale was the leader of the Sikh organization Damdami Taksal (Sikh educational organization), and a supporter of the Anandpur Resolution (proposing sovereignty of Sikhs).[ccclxxiii] In 1978, a group of Amritdhari Sikhs went to protest a reformist group of Sikhs (Nirankari). Resulting violence led to the death of thirteen Sikhs. After a series of events of civil disobedience, Bhindranwale and his followers set up base in the Golden Temple Complex in Punjab, India. In 1984, Prime Minister Indira Gandhi decided to establish control over the Golden Temple Complex and remove the militant religious leader Bhindranwale and his armed followers from the complex in what was called Operation Blue Star.

Hamandir Sahib or Darbar Sahib (also known as the Golden Temple). The holiest shrine in Sikhism located in the city of Amritsar, India.[ccclxxiv]

In 1984, Indira Gandhi was assassinated by two Sikh security guards in New Delhi in retaliation for Operation Blue Star. The assassination triggered violence against Sikhs across north India.

ISIS

The Islamic State in Iraq and Syria (ISIS) claims to be a fundamentalist Sunni group. It claims religious, political, and military authority over all Muslims worldwide.[ccclxxv] It follows an extremist interpretation of Islam, promotes religious violence, and regards Muslims who do not agree with its interpretation as infidels or apostates. ISIS proposes the foundation of a Sunni Islamic state and all those that do not believe in the group's interpretation of the Quran are to be killed. ISIS compels people in the areas that it controls to live according to its interpretation of Sharia law. There have been reports of the group's use of death threats, torture, and mutilation to compel conversion to Islam. ISIS has killed several thousand civilians of religious and minority groups including those of Yazidis (non-Muslims, ethnically Kurdish) and Shia Turkmen. Former US Secretary of State John Kerry stated that "...[ISIS] kills Christians because they are Christians; Yazidis because they are Yazidis; Shia because they are Shia."[ccclxxvi] In 2014, ISIS captured the Iraqi city of Mosul, demanding that all of the city's Christian inhabitants pay jizya (tax levied on non-Muslim subjects) and live as second-class citizens. Two days later, however, ISIS reneged on this promise of security, instead saying that Christians would be killed or forced to convert to Islam if they did not leave Mosul by the following week.

In Mosul, ISIS has implemented a Sharia school curriculum, which bans the teaching of art, music, national history, literature, and Christianity. After capturing cities in Iraq, ISIS issued guidelines on how to wear clothes and veils. ISIS warned women in the city of Mosul to wear full-face veils or face severe punishment. There are many reports of sexual abuse and enslavement in ISIS-controlled areas of women and girls, predominantly from the minority Christian and Yazidi communities. Fighters are told that they are free to have sex with or rape non-Muslim captive women. ISIS claims that the Quran allows fighters to have sex with captives, including adolescent girls, and to beat slaves as discipline.

Discussion

We have seen believers of one religion, or a version of the same religion often persecute either non-believers or persons considered as heretics (incorrectly interpreting the same religion). Persecution is sometimes a convenient way of providing punishment to people considered as "other" than those in your group. Those who persecute often believe they are cleansing their religion from errors that might distort their belief system. Persecuting or killing of teachers of other religions can be considered by some as silencing or eliminating false teachers, who could lead to the damnation of souls or disunity in the population. Persecutors not only can justify evil actions but may benefit financially from damaging others. Possessions of those persecuted are sometime confiscated by the religious authorities. Intolerance of other religions is largely seen by those who believe that they have the one and only truth.

Chapter 5 Religious Wars

Some may claim that religion has a positive influence on society and that religious people tend to be moral. The opposite is sometimes true. While wars are waged for many reasons, a common justification for war is religion. In some cases, the war is one religion against another while sometimes the war between factions within a religion (i.e. Protestants against Catholics or Sunnis against Shias). In some scenarios, it may be difficult to separate the various reasons or justifications for wars, but in the following we will examine some religiously motivated or justified wars that have been waged during history.

Jewish Warfare (2000 BCE-present)

There are many texts in the Old Testament that discuss where God instructed the Israelites to kill neighboring civilizations including the Amalekites, Amorites, Canaanites, Midianites, Hittite, Perizzites, Moabites, and Philistines.[ccclxxvii] The killing of these people was to often include men, women, and children. Jewish armies were led out to war by a special kohen[ccclxxviii] (priest), who was designated for this task. He would encourage the soldiers to fight bravely, telling them that God was on their side.

Some strains of radical Zionism promote aggressive war and justify them with biblical texts. Zionism is the national movement of the Jewish people that supports the re-establishment of a Jewish homeland in the territory defined as the historic Land of Israel[ccclxxix]. On May 14, 1948, the Jewish Agency, led by David Ben-Gurion, declared the creation of the State of Israel, and the same day the armies of seven Arab countries invaded Israel. The conflict led to an exodus of about 711,000 Palestinian Arabs. Later, a series of laws passed by the first Israeli government prevented Palestinians from returning to their homes, or claiming their property. The flight and expulsion of the Palestinians has since been widely, and controversially, described as having involved ethnic cleansing. The current Israeli-Palestinian conflict is often considered a war between Jews and Muslims.

Muslim Conquests (624-present)

The Muslims have spread their religion by conquests beginning in the lifetime of Muhammad and subsequent centuries. Muhammad began with battles against the polytheistic Arabs. There were periods of infighting among the Muslims from the seventh to eleventh centuries before the collapse of the Caliphate (state under the leadership of religious leader called a caliph). Jihad in the Quran was originally intended against Muhammad's local enemies, the pagans of Mecca, or the Jews of Medina, but the Quranic statements supporting jihad was redirected once new enemies appeared. Major battles in the history of Islam arose between the Meccans and the Muslims. One of the most important of these battles was the Battle of Badr in 624 CE.[ccclxxx] The Muslims were outnumbered by the Meccans by about 400 to 1000. The Muslim victory over the Meccan polytheists is claimed to be a demonstration of divine guidance and intervention on behalf of Muslims. The Quran states:

> "Allah had helped you at Badr, when ye were a contemptible little force; then fear Allah; thus, may ye show your gratitude."[ccclxxxi] Quran 3:123

Although, President George W. Bush stated, as have others, that Islam is a religion of peace, this is not consistent with the history of Islam or the Quran.[ccclxxxii]

Battle of Badr[ccclxxxiii]

Sunnis Against Shias (632-present)

Conflicts between the Sunnis and Shias stem from differences of opinion on who should have been the caliph after the death of Muhammad. Those who supported Abu Bakr came to be known as Sunni. Those who supported Muhammed's son-in-law, Ali came to be known as Shia.[ccclxxxiv] The daughter of Abu Bakr, Aisha, went to battle against Ali in Iraq at the Battle of the Camel. Mu'awiya, the Muslim governor of Damascus went to battle against Ali. Mu'awiya assumed the caliphate and founded the Ummayad Dynasty. Ali's son, Hussein went to battle with Mu'awiya's son Yazid. Hussein was killed and is considered a Shiite martyr. Sunni Muslims base their theological foundations on schools of Islamic jurisprudence. Shiites rely on spiritual leaders called Imams, which they believe are divinely appointed.[ccclxxxv]

Sunnis and Shiites fought in many conflicts including between the Sunni Ottoman Empire and the Shiite Shah of Persia. The Sunni Saudi Salafi sheiks were convinced that it was their religious mission to wage Jihad against all other forms of Islam. The Saudi Wahhabists under Abdul Aziz bin Muhammad bin Saud (ruled Saudi State 1765-1803)[ccclxxxvi] attacked and captured the holy Shia cities of Karbala and Najaf in Iraq, massacred the Shiites and destroyed Shiite tombs. They massacred thousands of the Shia population and stole enough property to load 4,000 camels. In 1802, they overtook Taif (city in Saudi Arabia). In 1803 and 1804 the Wahhabis overtook Mecca and Medina.

The Iran (Shia)-Iraq (Sunni) war[ccclxxxvii] resulted in at least half a million casualties and several billion dollars' worth of damages. Started by Iraq dictator Saddam Hussein in September 1980, the war was marked by indiscriminate ballistic-missile attacks, extensive use of chemical weapons and attacks on third-country oil tankers in the Persian Gulf. Hussein's (son of Ali, son-in-law of Muhammed) willingness to die on the battlefield was held up as a role model during Iran's war against Iraq from 1980 to 1988.[ccclxxxviii]

Jihad Against Hindus (1024-1030) - *discussed previously under persecution*

Sir Jadunath Sarkar[ccclxxxix] (Indian Bengali historian, 1870-1958) contends that several Muslim invaders were waging a systematic Jihad against Hindus in India to the effect that "Every device short of massacre in cold blood was resorted to convert heathen subjects." The Shiva idol at the Somnath temple was destroyed in a raid by Mahmud Ghazni in 1024 CE, which was considered the first act of Jihad in India. In addition to looting money Mahmud of Ghazni wanted to destroy Hindu temples and spread Islam in India.

Mahmud of Ghazni (CE 97-1030)[cccxc]

Crusades (~1096-1272)

The crusades were a series of religious wars undertaken by the Latin Church that predominately took place between the 11th and 13th centuries[cccxci]. The crusades were fought to capture Jerusalem, recapture Christian territory, and defend Christians in non-Christian lands. There were a series of crusades, which generally were at cross purposes with the original need to support the Christian Byzantines (Romans) in Constantinople. This effort to support Constantinople was sold to the people of Europe as an effort to recapture Jerusalem for the support of Christianity. This goal portrayed the crusade as an armed pilgrimage to the holy land for the support of fellow Christians, who had lost their land and were under Muslim rule. The Pope offered indulgences, full remission of sins, as an inducement for those who participated. The first crusade was successful in taking Jerusalem from the Muslims. The third crusade was the most famous in that Richard the Lionheart went to battle with Saladin. Richard had military victories but did not recapture Jerusalem.

Holy Family Catholic Church - Knight[cccxcii]

By the time of the fourth crusade the relations between the church in the west (Roman Catholic) and the east (Greek Orthodox) were so poor that the crusade ended up in the sack of Constantinople (one of the strongest cities in Christendom). Additional minor crusades were supported by the Pope in Rome, who used crusades to purify the beliefs of the church. There were additional crusades that were aimed at restoring Jerusalem to Christian control, which all failed. Basically, the crusades were the manipulation of Christians by the church to mobilize military forces by promise of eternal life to the participants. Many people died in these wars both as Christians against Muslims and Christians against Christians. These wars are an example of how people in power such as popes can use religion as a vehicle to attempt to attain their end goals but to the detriment of mankind.

Jihad Against Crusades (1169-1187)

European crusaders re-conquered much of the territory seized by the Islamic state, dividing it into four states, including the

Principality of Antioch, County of Tripoli, County of Edessa, and the Kingdom of Jerusalem.[cccxciii,cccxciv]

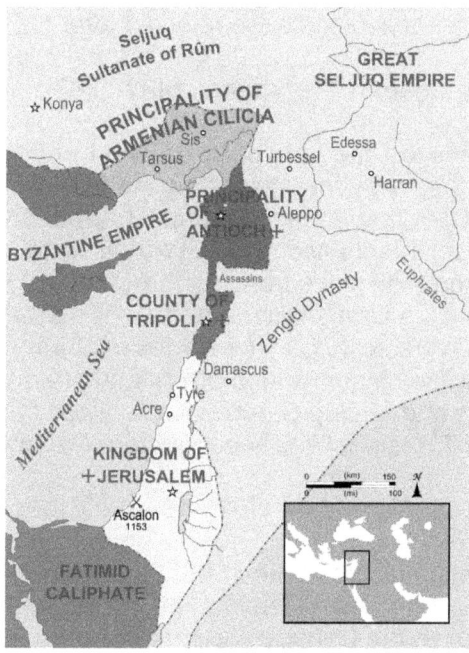

Crusader States 1165[cccxcv]

The Crusades originally had the goal of recapturing Jerusalem and the Holy Land from Muslim rule and were originally launched in response to a call from the Eastern Orthodox Byzantine Empire for help against the expansion of the Muslim Seljuk Turks into Anatolia. Initially, there was little effort to retake the lands from the crusaders, except for a few attacks made by the Egyptian Fatimids. This changed with the Imad ad-Din Zengi (ruler of what is today northern Iraq), who was the first emir to successfully repel the crusaders[cccxcvi]. He took Edessa, which triggered the Second Crusade, which was little more than a 47-year stalemate. The stalemate ended with the victory of Saladin over the forces of Jerusalem at the Horns of Hattin in 1187.[cccxcvii] While amassing his armies in Syria, Saladin had to create a doctrine, which would unite his forces and make them fight until the bitter end, which would be the only way they could re-conquer the lands taken in the First Crusade. Anyone who would abandon the Jihad would be committing a sin that could not be washed away by any means.[cccxcviii] Much of Saladin's teachings were rejected after his death.

Muslim Piracy Against Christians (1492-1587)

After the Muslims lost the area of Spain and Portugal they named it, El-Andalus, the name for "stolen," as the territory was hoped to be retrieved. The Spanish reconquered Granada from the Moors in 1492 and many Moors fled to North Africa. After attacks against Spanish shipping took place from North Africa, the Spanish retaliated by seizing Oran, Algiers, and Tunis. By 1518, the Muslim pirates were serving in the navies of North African Sultans, conducting activities that included attacks on enemy (especially Christian) trade and raiding European coastlines for potential slaves. By 1587, their activity became more like traditional piracy.

Muslims Against Christians (1520-1530)

Suleiman the Magnificent (1494-1566) began a series of military conquests in Europe. As sultan in 1520, he began his reign with campaigns against the Christian powers in central Europe and the Mediterranean. Belgrade fell to him in 1521 and Rhodes in 1522–23. In 1526, he defeated Louis II of Hungary. Religion was incorporated in the state structure, and the Sultan was regarded as "the protector of Islam." His Ottoman Empire was united by the Islamic warrior code with the aim of increasing Muslim territory through Jihad. Non-Muslims in parts of the empire had to provide some of their children as a tax. Conquered Christian communities, especially in the Balkans, had to surrender twenty percent of their male children to the state. These children were converted to Islam and served as slaves.

Suleiman in a portrait attributed to Titian c.1530[cccxcix]

The Ottoman Empire became the preeminent power in South-Eastern Europe. At its peak, the Ottoman Empire included Turkey, Egypt, Greece, Bulgaria, Romania, Macedonia, Hungry, Palestine, Jordan, Lebanon, Syria, parts of Arabia, and much of the coastal strip of North Africa.

German Peasants' War (1524-1525)

This was is also known as the Great Peasants' Revolt was fought in German majority areas of Europe between the Peasant army and Swabian League. German Peasants' war started in 1524 when King of France implemented different taxes on the Dutch churches as compared to the French churches and the rules for Dutch Catholics were also different. This fight resulted into the killing of more than 200,000 poor farmers and untrained soldiers and at the end, in 1525, the war was stopped, and all the participants were hanged till death.

Muslims Against Hindus (1527-1707) - *also discussed under persecution)*

In 1527, the Muslim leader, Zahiruddin Muhammad Babur,[cd] ordered a Jihad against the Hindu Rajputs (led by Rana Sanga) at the battle of Khanwa.[cdi] Publicly addressing his men, he declared the forthcoming battle a Jihad. His soldiers were facing a non-Muslim army for the first time ever. This was their chance to become either a soldier of Islam or a Martyr of Islam.

The Mughal emperor Aurangzeb (ruled from 1658-1707)[cdii] was considered a religious fanatic who sought to oppress Hindus. Aurangzeb ruled as a militant orthodox Sunni Muslim.[cdiii] He put through increasingly puritanical ordinances that were vigorously enforced by censors of morals. The Muslim confession of faith was removed from all coins so that it could not be defiled by unbelievers and courtiers were forbidden to salute in the Hindu fashion. Hindu idols, temples, and shrines were destroyed. Aurangzeb's harsh treatment of Hindus, and the reversal of the liberal religious policies of his predecessors have been cited as principal reasons for the disintegration of his empire.[cdiv]

Abyssinia – Somalia (1529-1559)

The Abyssinian–Adal war was a military conflict between the Abyssinians and the Muslim Adal Sultanate from 1529-1559.[cdv] The Imam Ahmad ibn Ibrahim al-Ghazi (considered as an ethnic Somali) came close to extinguishing the ancient realm of Abyssinia, and forcibly converting its surviving subjects to Islam.
The Portuguese, who had vested interests in the Indian Ocean, sent aid to the Abyssinians in the form of 400 musketeers. Adal, in response, received 900 from the Ottomans.[cdvi]

Ahmad ibn Ibrihim al-Ghazi[cdvii]

Both groups exhausted their resources and manpower in this conflict, allowing the northward migration of the Oromo (an ethnic group inhabiting Ethiopia and parts of Kenya and Somalia) into their present homelands to the north and west of Addis Ababa (Capital of Ethiopia).

Second War of Kappel (1531)

This religious war was a result of religious conflicts between Catholic cantons and Protestants during the reformation in Switzerland. In 1531 a force of approximately 7,000 soldiers from the five Catholic cantons met an army of only 2,000 men from Zürich at the Battle of Kappel. Zürich's army was unsupported by the other Protestant cantons and was led by Zwingli, while the combined Catholic army was led by Hans Jauch of Uri. When the fight was over, the victory was declared on the Catholic side and it was a rough that more than 700 people died including many civilians. A peace treaty led to Catholic and Protestant congregations worshiping in the same churches, which led to further tensions and conflicts throughout the sixteenth and seventeenth centuries.

The Battle of Kappel [cdviii]

Catholics and Protestants in Ireland (1534-present)

The history of Ireland involves the warring of Protestants and Catholics against each other. There are numerous incidents where Catholics or Protestants were killed solely because of their religion. There is a difficulty in separating actions of aggression based on religion from those based on nationality. Some argue that class is also a driving force, with the poor Catholic Irish rising up against the rich British Protestants. An examination of the main rebellions and wars reveal religion as the major, though not exclusive, factor.[cdix]

Almost as soon as England became Protestant there was a rebellion. In 1534 Silken Thomas (10th Earl of Kildare) hoped to gain the support of Catholics in his rebellion, but it was unsuccessful. In 1579, the Pope and the Spanish sent troops to help the Catholics in the Second Desmond Rebellion. The O'Neill's (including Hugh O'Neill, Earl of Tyrone) also received aid from Catholic Spain during the Nine Years War (1594-1603).

During the Irish rebellion of 1641, thousands of Protestants were massacred by Catholics because of their religion. The subsequent Irish Confederate Wars continued in Ireland until the 1650s.[cdx] In September 1649, Oliver Cromwell justified his sacking of Drogheda, Ireland as revenge for the massacres of Protestant settlers in Ulster, Ireland in 1641, calling the massacre "the righteous judgement of God on these barbarous wretches, who have imbrued their hands with so much innocent blood.[cdxi]"

The War of The Two Kings (1688-1691) was fought over whether the King would be a Catholic or a Protestant[cdxii]. This culminated in The Battle of the Boyne, which is celebrated to this day a victory of Protestants over Catholics. The Catholics received aid from France because both countries were Catholic. Following the war there were laws discriminating against Catholics solely because of their religion. These denied Catholics the right to vote and own land among other things. This was a clear attempt to divide the population based on religion.

The Irish Rebellion of 1798 was an uprising against British rule in Ireland.[cdxiii] The United Irishmen was an alliance of Methodists, Presbyterians, and Catholics against Anglicans. In Scullabogue, Ireland, 200 Protestants were locked in a barn and then set on fire. The rebels in Wexford were led by a Catholic priest, Father Murphy, which makes it hard to deny the role of religion. He was captured and brought before a military tribunal, charged with committing treason against the British crown, and sentenced to death. He was tortured to extract more information, stripped, flogged, hanged, decapitated, his corpse burnt in a barrel of tar, and his head impaled on a spike. Also, the Yeomanry, which suppressed the uprising was comprised of Protestant Irishmen, which shows it wasn't an entirely nationalist rebellion.

Irish Rebellion[cdxiv]

The War of Independence was claimed as nationalist wars, yet few Protestant Irishmen fought in the Irish Republican Army (IRA). The War of Independence was blatantly sectarian with thousands of Catholics burnt out of their homes. Note that they were persecuted based on religion not political ideology.

There is a wide debate over whether the war in Northern Ireland was a religious war with some arguing instead that its motivations were political. While this is true to an extent, it ignores the fact that people did not choose which side they were on. They were simply born into groups. You could not decide whether you were a Nationalist or a Unionist. This decision was already made for you based on what religion you were born into. Most of the killing was committed by sectarian paramilitaries who choose their victims based on religion and not on political beliefs. For example, in Kingsmill in 1976, a bus was stopped by the IRA. They did not ask the political opinions of the passengers, just whether they were Catholic or Protestant. The Protestants were then lined up and gunned down. The Ulster Volunteer Force would kill random Catholics on the street of Belfast. Bombs were planted in pubs based on the religion of its customers.

Religion has hugely affected Irish history. It has caused war, violence and the deaths of thousands. It has been a source of hatred and the prime divider of Irish society.

French Wars of Religion (1562-1598)

The French Wars of Religion continued from 1562-1598. These wars were between the Catholics and the Huguenots (Reformed/Calvinist Protestants) in the Kingdom of France. The fighting period ended in 1598 when the Huguenots or Protestants were granted the freedom and civil rights. There is no authentication to verify exactly how many wars were fought in this period and the real number of deaths in each war and historians are still researching on these perspectives as of this time. It is estimated that three million people perished in this period from violence, famine, or disease in what is considered the second deadliest religious war in European history (surpassed only by the Thirty Years' War, which took eight million lives)[cdxv].

This assassination of Coligny (Hugonet leader) by the Duke of Guise (Catholic) and his supporters began the series of events known as the St. Bartholomew's Day massacre. The city erupted as Catholics massacred Calvinist men, women and children and looted their houses. King Charles IX announced that he had ordered the massacre to prevent a Huguenot coup and proclaimed a day of jubilee in celebration even as the killings continued. The disorder spread to more than a dozen cities across France. Historians estimate that 2,000 Huguenots were killed in Paris and thousands more in the provinces; in all, perhaps 10,000 people were killed.

St. Bartholomew's Day Massacre[cdxvi]

Eighty Years' War (1568-1648)

Eighty Years' War is also known as independent war of Dutch and it was fought from 1568 to 1648 and it was fought in The Low Countries in between the Dutch and Spanish people. This was a victory for the Dutch as they got their own Republic of Dutch. There are numerous causes that led to the Eighty Years' War, but the primary reasons could be classified into two: resentment towards the Spanish authority and religious tension. A reason behind this 80-year long war was that Spain emperors implemented different religious rules in the entire Spanish dynasty including the provinces where Dutch were in majority. Religious resistance came with the imposition of an ecclesiastical hierarchy for all the Spanish territories. This created resistance in the Dutch provinces, which already embraced the Reformation.

Spanish Attack on a Flemish Village[cdxvii]

Thirty Year's War (1618-1648)

Thirty Years' War is a series of religious wars that were fought in between 1618 to 1648 in Europe and at that time, most of the European countries participated in these wars. This period of wars is the longest and most demolishing period of fighting in the history of the world that left more than 8 million deaths including soldiers and civilians. These short period wars were also fought between the religious conflicts in between the Holy Roman Empire and France, Sweden and Spain.

Barbary Wars (1801-1815)

The Barbary Wars[cdxviii] were a series of attacks by several Muslim nations on the coast of North Africa (Tunis, Tripoli, and Algiers) against Christian nations in Europe and America. Much of the Barbary activity was funded through the enslavement of European Christians. In the beginning of the seventeenth Century, there were more than 20,000 captives sold into slavery in Algiers alone. Although people from all over Christendom suffered Barbary attacks, the people who were the most likely victims were from Sicily. Any Christian nation that refused to pay tribute to Islam could have been subject to attack. In 1800, the Kingdom of Tripoli demanded an increase of tribute to prevent future attacks against the United States. However, the U.S. refused to pay the tribute, and this led to the First Barbary War. Jefferson and Adams wrote:

> "The Ambassador answered us, that (the aggression) was founded on the laws of their Prophet; that it was written in their Quran, that all nationals who should not have acknowledged their authority, were sinners; that it was their right and duty to make war upon them wherever they could be found, and to make slaves of all they could take as prisoners; and that every Mussulman who was slain in battle was sure to go to Paradise."[cdxix]

When the U.S. defeated the Tripolitanians in the Battle of Derne in 1805, the two nations signed a treaty that had favorable terms for the United States. A resurgence in Barbary attacks in 1815 led to the U.S. Navy being used again in the Second Barbary War, which also resulted in a U.S. victory and the ceasing of all Barbary attacks on American shipping without tribute.

Muslim Jihad Against Allied Powers in WWI (1914)

In 1914 the religious leader Sheikh-ul-Islam,[cdxx] declared Jihad on behalf of the Ottoman government, urging Muslims all over the world to take up arms against Britain, Russia, France, Serbia, and Montenegro in World War I. In this way, Muslims living under the sovereignty of Britain, France, Russia, Serbia, Montenegro and their supporters would deserve severe suffering, if they fought against Germany and Austria, who were helping the Ottoman government. The sheikh's declaration of a holy war urged Muslims all over the world to rise up and defend the Ottoman Empire, as a protector of Islam, against its enemies. "Of those who go to the Jihad for the sake of happiness and salvation of the believers in God's victory," the declaration read, "the lot of those who remain alive is felicity, while the rank of those who depart to the next world is martyrdom. In accordance with God's beautiful promise, those who sacrifice their lives to give life to the truth will have honor in this world, and their latter end is paradise.[cdxxi]"
Sheikh Hussein ibn Ali, the Emir of Mecca (1853-1931), refused to accommodate Ottoman requests that he endorse this jihad.

Pakistan and India (1947-present)

Communal violence in India includes acts of violence by followers of one religious group against followers and institutions of another religious group, often in the form of rioting.[cdxxii] After the dissolution of the British Raj in 1947, two new sovereign nations were formed: the Union of India and the Dominion of Pakistan. In the first Kashmir War, Islamic forces with support from the army of Pakistan attacked and occupied parts of Jammu and Kashmir forcing the Hindu Maharaja Hari Singh to sign accession of Jammu and Kashmir to the Dominion of India to obtain Indian military aid. The partition of the former British India displaced up to 12.5 million people, with estimates of loss of life varying from several hundred thousand to a million.[cdxxiii] India emerged as a secular nation with a Hindu majority, while Pakistan was established as an Islamic republic with Muslim majority population. There have been subsequent conflicts in 1965 (Indo-Pakistani War), 1971 (Bangladesh Liberation War), and 1999 (Kargil War)[cdxxiv].

Religious violence in India, especially in recent times, has generally involved Hindus and Muslims, although incidents of violence have also involved atheists, Christians, and Sikhs. There is also history of Muslim versus Parsee (adherents of Zoroastrianism) riots. Over 2005 to 2009, an average of 130 people died every year from communal violence. Over 2012, a total of 97 people died across India from various riots related to religious violence.

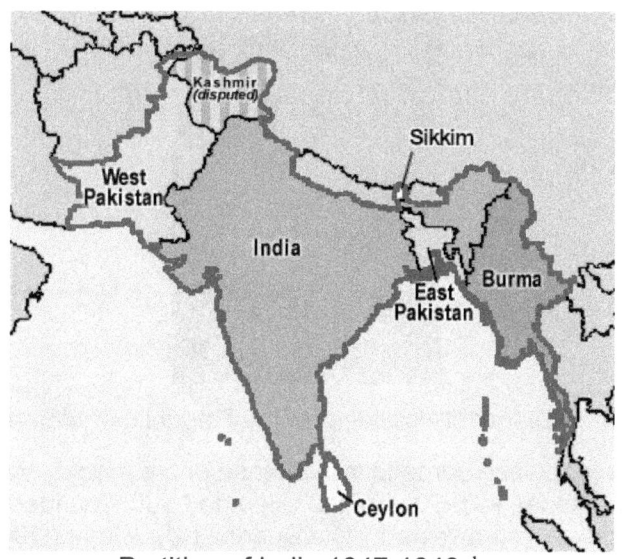

Partition of India 1947-1948[cdxxv]
(Note: East Pakistan is now Bangladesh)

Buddhist Uprising in Vietnam (1954-1966)

Ngo Dinh Diem was a catholic ruler in South Vietnam whose religious policies favored Catholics and persecuted many Buddhists. The distribution of weapons to village militias intended to repel Viet Kong guerrillas saw weapons given only to Catholics. Some Buddhist villages converted to receive aid or avoid being forcibly resettled by Diem's regime. In the heavily Buddhist central city of Hue, where Diem's elder brother was the Catholic Archbishop, the Buddhist majority was prohibited from displaying Buddhist flags during Vesak celebrations, which commemorated the birth of Gautama Buddha. The ban on religious flags led to a protest against the government, which was suppressed by Diem's forces and unarmed civilians were killed in the clash. A turning point came when a Buddhist monk set himself on fire in the middle of a busy Saigon intersection in protest of Diem's policies.

Ngo Dình Diem 1st President of the Republic of Vietnam[cdxxvi]

When the populace came to the defense of the monks, the resulting clashes saw 30 civilians killed and 200 wounded. In all 1,400 monks were arrested. The Buddhist Uprising of 1966 was a period of civil and military unrest in South Vietnam. In a country where the Buddhist majority was estimated to be between 70 and 90 percent, Diem ruled with a strong religious bias. As a member of the Catholic Vietnamese minority, he pursued pro-Catholic policies that antagonized many Buddhists.

First Sudanese Civil War (1955-1972)

This religious war was fought on the Sudan borders in between the military of Sudan and the Anyana guerrilla forces. It is estimated that about 10,000 soldiers participated from both sides and that it lasted from 1955 and to 1972. The Northern two-thirds of Sudan were overwhelmingly Muslim while Christianity or indigenous religions were most popular in the south. Northern Sudanese people spoke Arabic and identified with Saudi Arabia and North Africa while the Southerners looked to Ethiopia and the independent states of Sub-Saharan Africa. By the end of the war there were more than half a million deaths of soldiers and civilians. The country of Sudan remained in a tense peace for eleven years after the First Sudanese Civil War until a much larger and bloodier conflict called the Second Sudanese Civil War began in 1983[cdxxvii].

Lebanese Civil War (1975-1985)

Multiple factors including socioeconomic differences in the Sunni, Shiite, and Christian populations, distribution of political power, and regional events may have led to the Lebanese Civil War (1975-1985).[cdxxviii] The militarization of the Palestinian refugee population, with the arrival of the Palestinian Liberation Organization guerrilla forces sparked an arms race amongst the different Lebanese political factions. The conflict was between three religious lines, Sunni Muslim, Christian Lebanese, and Shiite Muslim.

It has been argued that the antecedents of the war can be traced back to the conflicts and political compromises reached after the end of Lebanon's administration by the Ottoman Empire. The Cold War had a powerful disintegrative effect on Lebanon, which was closely linked to the polarization that preceded the 1958 political crisis. During the 1948 Arab-Israeli War an exodus of Palestinian refugees who fled the fighting or were expelled from their homes, arrived in Lebanon. Palestinians came to play an important role in future Lebanese civil conflicts, while the establishment of Israel radically changed the local environment in which Lebanon found itself. Lebanon was promised independence and in 1943 it was achieved. French troops that had invaded Lebanon in 1941 to rid Beirut of the Vichy forces, left the country in 1946. The Christians assumed power over the country and economy. A confessional parliament was created, where Muslims and Christians were given quotas of seats in parliament. The President was to be a Christian, the Prime Minister a Sunni Muslim, and the Speaker of Parliament a Shia Muslim.

In 1991, parliament passed an amnesty law that pardoned all political crimes prior to its enactment. In 1991, the militias with the exception of Hezbollah were dissolved, and the Lebanese Armed Forces began to slowly rebuild themselves as Lebanon's only major non-sectarian institution. In 1991 a car bomb exploded in the Muslim neighborhood of Basta. At least thirty people were killed, and 120 wounded, including former Prime Minister Shafik Wazzan.

Second Sudanese War (1983-2005)

The Second Sudanese Civil War (1983-2005) is described as an ethnoreligious conflict where the Muslim central government's pursuits to impose Sharia law on non-Muslim southerners led to violence, and eventually to the civil war. The conflict was marked by violence against civilians, which caused the deaths of between 1 and 2 million civilians, many of which were a result of starvation and disease.

Sudan and now South Sudan have experienced decades of armed conflict with devastating impact on the civilian populations. Each phase of fighting has ended through mediation, followed by a short period of quiet, and then a new round of fighting, displacement, and death. Armies from all sides enlisted children in their ranks[cdxxix]. Following an internal outcry, the Sadiq al-Mahdi government in March 1989 agreed with the United Nations and donor nations on a plan called Operation Lifeline Sudan, under which some 100,000 tons of food was moved into Sudan, and widespread starvation was averted. The war resulted in the independence of South Sudan six years after the war ended. Sudan is Muslim and South Sudan is Christian.

Yugoslav Wars (1991-1995)

The Croatian War (1991–1995) and Bosnian War (1992–1995), have been viewed as religious wars between the Orthodox, Catholic, and Muslim populations of former Yugoslavia, that is, Serbs, Croats, and Bosnians, respectively. The Croatian War of Independence began when Serbs in Croatia, who were opposed to Croatian independence, announced their secession from Croatia following Croatia's declaration of independence. In 1992, conflict consumed Bosnia and Herzegovina. The war was predominantly a territorial conflict between the Republic of Bosnia and Herzegovina chiefly supported by Bosniaks, the self-proclaimed Bosnian Serb entity Republika Srpska, and the self-proclaimed Herzeg-Bosnia, who were led and supplied by Serbia and Croatia respectively, reportedly with a goal of the partition of Bosnia. Ethnic cleansing was a common phenomenon in the wars in Croatia, Kosovo and Bosnia and Herzegovina. This entailed intimidation, forced expulsion, or killing of the unwanted ethnic group as well as the destruction of the places of worship, cemeteries and cultural and historical buildings of that ethnic group to alter the population composition of an area in the favor of another ethnic group which would become the majority. War rape occurred as a matter of official orders as part of ethnic cleansing, to displace the targeted ethnic group[cdxxx].

Traditional religious symbols were used during the wars. Foreign Islamic jihadist fighters came to Bosnia as mujahedeen. According to the International Center for Transitional Justice, the Yugoslav Wars resulted in the death of 140,000 people.[cdxxxi]

Nigerian Conflict (1999-2015)

Following the return of democratic government in 1999, the Muslim-dominated northern Nigerian states have introduced Sharia law, including punishments against blasphemy and apostasy. Several incidents occurred in which people have been killed for or in response to perceived insults to Islam. Today, religious violence in Nigeria is dominated by the Boko Haram Islamic State in West Africa (ISWA) insurgency, which aims to impose Sharia on the northern parts of the country. Islamic fundamentalist groups, such as the Boko Haram, seek to return to the Islamic religion as described by Mohammed in the Quran.

Boko Haram[cdxxxii]

In 2012, tensions within Boko Haram resulted in gradual split of the group between Salafist (reform movement in Sunni Islam) conservative faction led by Abu Usmatul al-Ansari, and the more violent faction led by Abubakar Shekau. By 2015, part of the group split into al-Qaeda affiliated Ansaru, and Shekau's faction became Islamic State of Iraq (ISIL)'s West Africa branch. In 2013, over 1,000 people died as a result of the conflict. The violence increased in 2014 to 10,849 deaths.[cdxxxiii]

9/11 Attack on the Twin Towers (2001)

On September 11, 2001 members of al-Qaeda executed a terrorist attack on the United States. The attack included the destruction of the Twin Towers in New York City. Osama bin Laden declared a holy war against the United States. Al-Qaeda released a Fatwa stating:

> "We -- with God's help -- call on every Muslim who believes in God and wishes to be rewarded to comply with God's order to kill the Americans and plunder their money wherever and whenever they find it. We also call on Muslim ulema [Muslim scholars in sacred law and theology], leaders, youths, and soldiers to launch the raid on Satan's U.S. troops and the devil's supporters allying with them, and to displace those who are behind them so that they may learn a lesson."[cdxxxiv]

In Bin Laden's November 2002 letter to America, he states:

> "The creation and continuation of Israel is one of the greatest crimes, and you are the leaders of its criminals. And, of course, there is no need to explain and prove the degree of American support for Israel. The creation of Israel is a crime which must be erased. Each and every person whose hands have become polluted in the contribution towards this crime must pay its price, and pay for it heavily."[cdxxxv]

Osama Bin Laden

This act of violence is linked to religious motivation. Muslim martyrs were expecting to obtain reward in paradise for their service to Allah.

Discussion

A psychological strategy for waging war on others is to dehumanize the enemy. The emphasis on demonizing the enemy enables the combatants to justify their injuring and killing other human beings. Promising an afterlife and potential reward in that afterlife for participating in a "holy" war enables soldiers to be used as pawns in a war, where their lives can be lost. The soldiers themselves may be willing to be martyrs or act with increased ferocity or greater bravery in battle, since they may be able to act without fear of death. Thus, those who claim to be moral based on actions according to their religious beliefs are the same ones who joyfully have killed others in the name of their religion.

Conclusion

Religion developed as a theoretical method for obtaining favorable events during life and potentially in a future life. It provided a power structure and enabled cultural differentiation. Religion has evolved over time with fracture occurring as a function of dissatisfaction with the leadership and beliefs of the existing religions. New religions have provided alternative power structures for groups. Religions are generally passed on to relatives and neighbors.

Let us assume that some religion is true. If this were the case, then all other religions that have differences with that religion would at least be partially incorrect. Different religions have been formed or created over history by individuals or groups. Thus, most all religions have times of conception that are well after many people have lived and died. It seems odd that truth would be discovered or delivered to mankind after many have lived and died without knowledge of the true religion. Potentially the consequences of this lack of information could lead to eternal negative outcomes. Thus, it would seem that the only possible true religion would have to have been instituted by a God or gods at the beginning of mankind's existence. It is not clear what this religion would be, since all known religions have come into existence by the creation of men as evolved concepts from previous religions.

It appears probable (based on the paucity of evidence supporting the claims of religions as examined earlier) that all religions are false. While religions may have served some purposes in the past (helping to generate a culture and morality, encourage unity within a group, provide for authority of power, and aid in demonizing the enemy for effectiveness in warfare) they no longer serve beneficial functions in society. Religions have enabled an us/them psychology, which has been used and is still used to justify ill treatment of others. As society has matured in its scientific and moral sophistication, religion should be phased out of society because of its negative effects. Claims that religion provides a needed moral structure for society are unfounded. Religions disagree on what moral behavior is and the foundations for these beliefs are based on error.

There are already too many reasons such as ethnic, national, and cultural differences used to justify wars, prejudice, and persecution.

While it is stated in the New Testament that the love of money is the root of all evil, this is not the case in that money has not always existed and money is not always the motivation for evil deeds.

...the love of money is the root of all evil.... 1 Timothy 6:10[cdxxxvi]

The love of God can be a root of evil, since it is a belief that often leads to ill treatment of those who do not adhere to the religion's beliefs.

Perhaps it would be of value to consider religion from the aspect of an extraterrestrial or a naïve but intelligent observer. It may be challenging to explain why so many different beliefs or opinions exist on whether a God or gods exist and what this God or gods is like. Additionally, since there appears to be no way to prove the existence of a God or gods, it would be impossible to describe this unknown and unproven being. Since all ideas on this topic or religions are speculative, it would seem irrational to argue, ostracize, and kill people over varied opinions on a topic that is without proof.

Ironically, those that are religious often tend to be divided by relatively minor differences in their beliefs. It might be reasonable to conclude that in the absence of proof of existence, non-existence is likely. As we have no credible proof for the existence of unicorns, leprechauns, or fairies, we conclude that they do not exist. Similarly, we have no credible proof for the existence of any of the gods or God of the thousands of different religions. It seems inappropriate for people to accept religious dogma without rational, scientific, or logical reasoning. More ridiculous is for people who vary in opinion on these ideas to engage in argument or an attempt to persuade others to accept these irrational concepts with vehement fanaticism, sometimes to the point of violence.

A majority of people are caught up in religions, which exact time and resources that are wasted on these religions. Although none of the religions can substantiate their religion as being correct or true, and it can be seen that things such as heaven, hell, angels, virgin births, resurrections, and world-wide floods are mythological. Since many religious adherents have been indoctrinated for many years or may be shunned by believing family, they will usually not listen to reason. To appeal to their rational, logical understanding is offensive and largely leads to vehement disagreement and offense.[cdxxxvii] The scientific facts are in opposition to their worldview but "Once formed, impressions are remarkably perseverant.[cdxxxviii]" The only way that these adherents can rationalize supernatural, non-scientific doctrines of their religions is to appeal to the power of their unsubstantiated god. While I would like to think that the words of this book would help convince people of the truth related to religions, I am not optimistic that this is the case.

In conclusion, consider the lyrics from John Lennon's song "Imagine" in which he suggests that we image that there is no heaven, hell, or religion, but as opposed to "imagining" the absence of heaven and hell, I suggest we face reality. While religion is only one of the sources that can lead to conflict, ostracism, and bias, I conclude that it is an unnecessary legacy from our past superstitious beliefs. While many will disagree with this opinion, I hope that this book provides some information for consideration.

Acknowledgements

Thanks to my sons, Eric and Travis, as well as Michael Brown and Michael Nolin for their comments on initial drafts of the book.

Index

Abraham 20, 41, 104, 108
Ahura Mazda 17, 24, 25, 62
Allah36, 52, 69, 74, 75, 100, 102, 104, 105, 126, 158, 181
Angel.36, 102, 104, 106, 109, 126, 185
Anglican 168
Ashtoreth...................................18, 19
Aztec...85
Baal..18, 19
Baha'i 132
Bhindranwale.........................154, 155
Bible 34, 39, 48, 55, 65, 67, 73, 94, 100, 102, 103, 106, 108, 109, 131, 136, 152
Boko Haram............................179, 180
Buddha .28, 29, 59, 60, 61, 68, 69, 124
Buddhism13, 14, 17, 25, 26, 28, 29, 39, 45, 59, 68, 69, 77, 78, 109, 110, 113, 121, 124, 125, 131, 142, 146
Buddhist29, 59, 60, 77, 78, 92, 123, 124, 125, 129, 131, 137, 142, 145, 146, 175, 176
Cargo cults 86
Cathar...150
Catholic35, 73, 94, 120, 121, 122, 129, 130, 131, 138, 147, 150, 151, 152, 153, 157, 162, 167, 168, 169, 170, 175, 176, 178
Christian Scientists........................139
Christianity13, 14, 24, 33, 34, 35, 36, 45, 48, 67, 73, 75, 78, 80, 81, 86, 89, 99, 100, 101, 102, 106, 107, 108, 120, 121, 130, 135, 156, 161
Confucianism.................13, 17, 30, 31
Confucius 30, 31
Creator.........................57, 58, 101, 111
Crusade..................147, 161, 162, 163
David Koresh.............................91, 94
David Yonggi Cho............................91
Demon 62, 102, 108, 139
Digambara 26, 132
Durga..23
Four Noble Truths............................68

Free will................................24, 74, 107
Gaia 53
Ganesha 23
Gilgamesh............................54, 55, 65
God 1, 3, 13, 17, 20, 22, 27, 34, 36, 38, 39, 41, 42, 47, 48, 49, 50, 57, 63, 65, 66, 67, 68, 69, 70, 73, 74, 75, 80, 83, 85, 87, 97, 99, 100, 101, 102, 103, 106, 107, 108, 109, 111, 112, 113, 117, 119, 121, 123, 125, 126, 127, 134, 139, 157, 168, 173, 180, 183, 184
Great Spirit 58
Hades 19, 104, 113, 114
Haile Selassie 41, 42
Heaven24, 31, 34, 45, 48, 49, 55, 61, 62, 67, 73, 74, 77, 78, 79, 94, 98, 100, 103, 104, 106, 107, 144, 185
Hell 73, 74, 77, 103, 104, 105
Hindu13, 14, 17, 21, 22, 23, 39, 45, 63, 67, 68, 75, 76, 78, 81, 109, 113, 119, 125, 126, 131, 132, 133, 134, 135, 137, 138, 143, 145, 160, 165, 166, 174
Hinduism13, 14, 21, 22, 23, 39, 45, 63, 67, 75, 76, 78, 81, 109, 113, 125, 131, 132, 135, 137
Hindus...........22, 23, 67, 133, 145, 166
Hogen Fukunaga 91
Human sacrifice 85
ISIS 94, 155, 156
Islam13, 14, 24, 36, 37, 39, 45, 48, 69, 74, 75, 78, 81, 88, 89, 95, 99, 100, 101, 102, 106, 117, 120, 121, 122, 123, 126, 130, 131, 132, 133, 135, 138, 145, 149, 155, 158, 159, 160, 162, 164, 165, 166, 172, 173, 174, 179, 180
Jainism14, 25, 26, 45, 109, 110, 113, 132, 142
Jehovah Witnesses 139
Jerry Falwell 92

189

Jesus 33, 34, 40, 100, 103, 104, 106, 107, 108, 109, 130
Jewish 95, 102, 107, 133, 134, 147, 151, 157
Jews 20, 21, 127, 132, 134, 137, 147, 148, 157, 158
Jihad 158, 159, 160, 162, 164, 165, 173
Jim Bakker 96
Jim Jones 91
John Calvin 35, 83
John Smyth 35
John Wesley 35
Joseph Smith 39, 40, 89
Judaism 14, 17, 20, 24, 33, 34, 36, 45, 48, 81, 89, 99, 101, 102, 104, 127, 128, 130, 131, 135, 138, 142, 147, 148, 149, 193
Karma 23, 26, 28, 39, 60, 75, 77, 78, 110, 111, 113, 123, 125, 143
L. Ron Hubbard 91, 95
Latter Day Saints 40, 136
Madrasa 120
Mahayana 29, 77
Manichaeists 146
Marcus Garvey 41
Martin Luther 35, 89, 97, 147
Mayan 84, 85
Methodist 35, 168
Missions 121
Moral Majority 92, 97
Mormon 39, 40, 89, 128, 130, 136, 137
Muhammad 36, 37, 100, 121, 158, 159, 165
Muslims 36, 70, 74, 102, 123, 132, 136, 137, 145, 147, 155, 157, 158, 159, 161, 162, 164, 173, 174, 177
Near death experiences. 82, 106, 107
Nirvana 30, 110
Noble Eightfold Path 30, 69
Oneida Community 128, 129
Oral Roberts 91, 96
Orthodox ... 35, 131, 147, 162, 163, 178
Paradise 106, 126, 173
Paul Schäfer 91
Poseidon 19

Prayer 20, 99
Predestined 107
Presbyterian 35, 168
Protestant 35, 73, 89, 147, 151, 153, 157, 167, 168, 169, 170
Purpose of life 24, 47, 66, 67, 68, 69, 70, 72
Quran 36, 51, 52, 55, 65, 69, 70, 75, 100, 102, 103, 104, 105, 106, 123, 126, 127, 128, 134, 155, 156, 158, 179
Rastafarianism 41
Reincarnation 23, 26, 39, 41, 45, 61, 68, 75, 77, 112, 113, 121, 138, 141, 151
Rigveda 63
Satan 106
Sati 134
Scientology 91, 95, 96, 139
Shakers 129
Sharia 92, 123, 130, 155, 156, 178, 179
Sheol 104
Shia 37, 155, 157, 159, 177
Shiite 159, 177
Shintoism 32, 139, 142
Shoko Asahara 91
Sikh 14, 38, 39, 45, 81, 109, 111, 112, 113, 133, 145, 154, 155, 174
Sikhism 14, 38, 39, 45, 81, 109, 111, 113, 133
Sin 73, 80, 100, 106, 107, 123, 125, 126, 127, 130, 132, 136, 137, 161, 173
Spanish inquisition 152
Suleiman 164, 165
Sunni 37, 130, 155, 157, 159, 166, 177, 180
Svetambara 26, 132
Taoism 13, 17, 27, 28, 131
Taoist 27, 28, 131, 146
Theravada 29, 77
Torah 20, 21, 100, 102, 106
Unitarian 132
Upanishad 21, 64
Vishnu 22, 23, 65
Waldensian 150
Wicca 42, 132

Witch 43, 152, 153, 154
Zeus 19
Zionism 157
Zoroaster 24
Zoroastrianism 24, 25, 62, 174
Zoroastrians 17, 24, 146

About the author:

The author has a BS and MS in electrical engineering and a Ph.D. in engineering. He worked for a medical device manufacturer Texas and as a government contractor in Maryland. He was an adjunct professor of electrical engineering and high school teacher of physics. He works for the Department of Health and Human Services. He has written on the effects of electromagnetic fields on the electroencephalogram, name matching algorithms, and kinetic therapy. Dr. Bell served as a deacon and a Sunday school teacher in several protestant churches.

Back Cover

Image of Gustave Dore crusades entry of the crusaders into Constantinople.

Public Domain,
https://commons.wikimedia.org/w/index.php?curid=123885

Endnotes

Part 1 – Origin, Purpose, and Validity of Religion

Chapter 1 Origin of Religions

[i] Dictionary - Google Search
[ii] Clifford Geertz, Religion as a Cultural System, 1973
[iii] https://www.irs.gov/pub/irs-tege/eotopica94.pdf
[iv] World Religion Statistics Geography Church Statistics, 2015
[v] http://www.adherents.com/Religions_By_Adherents.html
[vi] https://upload.wikimedia.org/wikipedia/commons/6/60/Worldwide_percentage_of_Adherents_by_Religion.png, public domain
[vii] Breaking the Spell – Religion as a Natural Phenomenon, Daniel C. Dennett 2006
[viii] https://en.wikipedia.org/wiki/Major_religious_groups#/media/File:World_religions_map_en.svg, public domain
[ix] http://www.ancient-origins.net/ancient-places-europe/venus-figurines-european-paleolithic-era-001548
[x] http://www.ancient-origins.net/ancient-places-europe/venus-figurines-european-paleolithic-era-001548, permission granted 21 September 2018
[xi] https://www.newscientist.com/article/mg22530134-200-red-lady-cave-burial-reveals-stone-age-secrets/
[xii] https://infogalactic.com/info/Proto-Indo-European_religion
[xiii] http://www.bbc.co.uk/history/ancient/egyptians/primary_sources_01.shtml
[xiv] http://www.crystalinks.com/pyramidtext.html - permission granted 16 Sept 2018
[xv] http://news.bbc.co.uk/2/hi/science/nature/7625145.stm
[xvi] Sarah Iles Johnston (2004). Religions of the Ancient World: A Guide. Harvard University Press. p. 206.
[xvii] https://www.allaboutreligion.org/origin-of-religion.htm
[xviii] http://realhistoryww.com/world_history/ancient/Misc/Elam/Zoroastrian_rel.htm
[xix] https://commons.wikimedia.org/wiki/File:Religion_timeline_graph.jpg, public domain
[xx] http://www.mc.maricopa.edu/~thoqh49081/StudentPapers/canaanite.html
[xxi] https://www.gaychristian101.com/Shrine-Prostitutes.html, permission granted 16 Sept 2018
[xxii] Annette Reed (11 February 2005). "Life, Death, and Afterlife in Ancient Israel and Canaan"
[xxiii] Segal, Alan F. Life after death: a history of the afterlife in the religions of the West
[xxiv] https://en.wikipedia.org/wiki/Ancient_Greek_religion
[xxv] Beginnings of Judaism by The Great Courses (Author), The Great Courses (Publisher) The Great Courses (2013)
[xxvi] File: Jerusalem Modell BW 3.JPG, public domain
[xxvii] http://bethadonai.com/?page_id=511
[xxviii] https://rsc.byu.edu/archived/temple-antiquity-ancient-records-and-modern-perspectives/temple-and-synagogue

[xxix] Michaels, Axel *(2004), Hinduism. Past and present*, Princeton, New Jersey: Princeton University Press
[xxx] Bilimoria; et al., eds. (2007). Indian Ethics: Classical Traditions and Contemporary Challenges. p. 103.
[xxxi] http://www.discovervedanta.com/index.htm
[xxxii] David Lawrence (2012), The Routledge Companion to Theism (Editors: Charles Taliaferro, Victoria S. Harrison and Stewart Goetz), Routledge, ISBN 978-0415881647, pages 78-79
[xxxiii] https://en.wikipedia.org/wiki/Vishnu#/media/File:Bhagavan_Vishnu.jpg, public domain
[xxxiv] https://www.brooklynmuseum.org/opencollection/objects/127710, public domain
[xxxv] https://pixabay.com/en/ganesha-parvathi-devi-madurai-1576096/, free for commercial use
[xxxvi] https://he.m.wikipedia.org/wiki/קובץ:Zartosht_30salegee.jpg, public domain
[xxxvii] http://content.time.com/time/world/article/0,8599,1864931,00.html
[xxxviii] https://en.wikipedia.org/wiki/File:Faravahar-Gold.svg, public domain
[xxxix] http://www.bbc.co.uk/religion/religions/jainism/ataglance/glance.shtml
[xl] https://www.britannica.com/topic/Jainism
[xli] http://guides.lib.uw.edu/research/Jainism, permission granted 21 September 2018
[xlii] http://www.qcc.cuny.edu/SocialSciences/ppecorino/PHIL_of_RELIGION_TEXT/CHAPTER_2_RELIGIONS/Jainism.htm
[xliii] https://www.jainworld.com/jainbooks/antiquity/digasvet.htm
[xliv] Pollard; Rosenberg; Tignor, Elizabeth; Clifford; Robert (2011). Worlds Together Worlds Apart. New York, New York: Norton. p. 164.
[xlv] http://www.religionfacts.com/taoism
[xlvi] https://www.ancient.eu/Taoism/
[xlvii] https://commons.wikimedia.org/wiki/File:Laozi_002.jpg, public domain
[xlviii] http://www.chebucto.ns.ca/Philosophy/Taichi/gods.html
[xlix] http://www.bbc.co.uk/religion/religions/taoism/ataglance/glance.shtml
[l] http://fengshuigate.com/zangshu.html
[li] https://commons.wikimedia.org/wiki/File:Buddha_in_Sarnath_Museum_(Dhammajak_Mutra).jpg, public domain
[lii] http://www.pewforum.org/2012/12/18/global-religious-landscape-buddhist/
[liii] https://commons.wikimedia.org/wiki/File:Buddhism_percent_population_in_each_nation_World_Map_Buddhist_data_by_Pew_Research.svg, public domain
[liv] Gethin, Rupert (1998), Foundations of Buddhism, Oxford University Press
[lv] Fung, Yiu-ming (2008), "Problematizing Contemporary Confucianism in East Asia", in Richey, Jeffrey, Teaching Confucianism, Oxford University Press
[lvi] https://commons.wikimedia.org/wiki/File:Half_Portraits_of_the_Great_Sage_and_Virtuous_Men_of_Old_-_Confucius.jpg, public domain
[lvii] https://www.britannica.com/topic/Confucianism
[lviii] http://www.dbschlosser.com/five-virtues-of-confucius/
[lix] John Nelson. A Year in the Life of a Shinto Shrine. 1996. pp. 7–8.
[lx] https://www.gotquestions.org/Shintoism.html

lxi http://www.bbc.co.uk/religion/religions/shinto/ataglance/glance.shtml
lxii http://www.bbc.co.uk/religion/religions/shinto/history/emperor_1.shtml
lxiii https://worldreligions.wordpress.ncsu.edu/shintoism/
lxiv https://www.deliriumsrealm.com/izanami/
lxv
https://upload.wikimedia.org/wikipedia/commons/2/2e/Oomatono_Tsunoten_Shinto_Shrine_in_Inagi_taken_in_May_2009.jpg, public domain
https://commons.wikimedia.org/wiki/File:Pietro_Perugino_040.jpg, public domain
lxvii https://commons.wikimedia.org/wiki/File:Rome-Capitole-StatueConstantin.jpg, public domain
lxviii https://en.wikipedia.org/wiki/Chalcedonian_Definition
lxix Gourley, Bruce. "A Very Brief Introduction to Baptist History, Then and Now." The Baptist Observer.
lxx
https://commons.wikimedia.org/wiki/File:Mohammed_receiving_revelation_from_the_angel_Gabriel.jpg, public domain
lxxi http://edition.cnn.com/2015/04/02/living/pew-study-religion/
lxxii http://www.newworldencyclopedia.org/entry/Battle_of_Karbala
lxxiii https://isla.uga.edu/ibadis.html
lxxiv https://commons.wikimedia.org/wiki/File:Madhhab_Map_(Divisions_of_Islam).png, public domain
lxxv The preaching of Islam: a history of the propagation of the Muslim faith By Sir Thomas Walker Arnold, pp.125-126
lxxvi Luis Moreno; César Colino (2010). Diversity and Unity in Federal Countries. McGill Queen University Press. p. 207
lxxvii Dawe, Donald G. "Srī Gurū Nānak Dev". Encyclopaedia of Sikhism. Punjabi University Patiala.
lxxviii https://en.m.wikipedia.org/wiki/File:GuruNanakFresco-Goindwal.jpg, public domain
lxxix https://www.sikhs.org/granth.htm
lxxx https://karnataka.pscnotes.com/main-notes/paper-ii-general-studies-1/sikhism-principles-practices-evolution/
lxxxi https://www.britannica.com/biography/Arjan
lxxxii http://www.sikhiwiki.org/index.php/Guru_Tegh_Bahadur
lxxxiii https://www.sikhs.org/khalsa.htm
lxxxiv
http://www.realsikhism.com/index.php?subaction=showfull&id=1250025675&ucat=5
lxxxv http://www.bbc.co.uk/religion/religions/mormon/beliefs/christian.shtml
lxxxvi https://www.mormonnewsroom.org/article/brigham-young
lxxxvii
https://commons.wikimedia.org/wiki/File:Joseph_Smith,_Jr._portrait_owned_by_Joseph_Smith_III.jpg, public domain
lxxxviii Church Educational System (1996, rev. ed.). Book of Mormon Student Manual (Salt Lake City, Utah: The Church of Jesus Christ of Latter-day Saints), ch. 6.
lxxxix http://www.religionfacts.com/mormonism/afterlife
xc http://www.bbc.co.uk/religion/religions/rastafari/ataglance/glance.shtml
xci https://en.wikipedia.org/wiki/Marcus_Garvey#/media/File:Marcus_Garvey_1924-08-

05.jpg, public domain
[xcii] https://cs.m.wikipedia.org/wiki/Soubor:Addis_Ababa-8e00855u.jpg, public domain
[xciii] https://en.wikipedia.org/wiki/Gerald_Gardner_(Wiccan)
[xciv] https://en.wikipedia.org/wiki/Triple_Goddess_(Neopaganism)
[xcv] http://dotconnectoruk.blogspot.com/2010/04/is-raelian-cult-signaling-illuminati.html
[xcvi] https://www.dailymail.co.uk/femail/article-2624420/Inside-wacky-world-Ra-lians-cult-believes-humans-descended-ALIENS.html
[xcvii] https://raelusa.org/raelian-movement/
[xcviii] https://raelusa.org/raelian-movement/

Chapter 2 – Key Questions Addressed by Religion

[xcix] https://www.Biblegateway.com/passage/?search=Genesis+1&version=NIV
[c] https://www.space.com/25126-big-bang-theory.html
[ci] Planck Collaboration (2015). "Planck 2015 results. XIII. Cosmological parameters (See PDF, page 32, Table 4, Age/Gyr, last column)". Astronomy & Astrophysics. 594
[cii] Bennett, C.L.; et al. (2013). "Nine-Year Wilkinson Microwave Anisotropy Probe (WMAP) Observations: Final Maps and Results". The Astrophysical Journal Supplement Series. 208
[ciii] https://astrosociety.org/edu/publications/tnl/56/ancient3.html
[civ] http://humanorigins.si.edu/education/introduction-human-evolution
[cv] https://en.wikipedia.org/wiki/Human_evolution
[cvi] https://www.ncbi.nlm.nih.gov/books/NBK230201/
[cvii] https://commons.wikimedia.org/wiki/File:Timeline_evolution_of_life.svg, public domain
[cviii] Hesiod, Theogony, 116–138
[cix] http://www.ancient-literature.com/greece_hesiod_theogony.html
[cx] Krstovic, Jelena O., ed. (2005). Epic of Gilgamesh Classical and Medieval Literature Criticism. 74
[cxi] https://commons.wikimedia.org/wiki/File:The_Newly_Discovered_Tablet_V_of_the_Epic_of_Gilgamesh._Meeting_Humbaba,_with_Enkidu,_at_the_Cedar_Forest._The_Sulaymaniyah_Museum,_Iraqi_Kurdistan.jpg, public domain
[cxii] https://ncse.com/library-resource/yes-noahs-flood-may-have-happened-not-over-whole-earth
[cxiii] https://ncse.com/cej/4/1/impossible-voyage-noahs-ark
[cxiv] Weaver, Jace (2001). Other Words: American Indian Literature, Law, and Culture. Oklahoma University Press. pp. 164–172
[cxv] http://www.americanyawp.com/reader/the-new-world/indian-creation-stories/
[cxvi] http://www.indians.org/welker/creation.htm
[cxvii] http://www.indigenouspeople.net/creation.htm
[cxviii] http://coursesite.uhcl.edu/HSH/Whitec/texts/Amerind/origins/AmindorsIroquois.htm
[cxix] http://historymatters.gmu.edu/d/6375/
[cxx] https://pib.socioambiental.org/en/Povo:Xingu
[cxxi] https://pib.socioambiental.org/en/Povo:Yawalapiti
[cxxii] https://www.budsas.org/ebud/whatbudbeliev/297.htm

cxxiii http://vasudhaivakutumbakama.blogspot.com/2017/03/buddhist-concepts-of-universe.html
cxxiv https://www.lionsroar.com/what-are-the-12-niddanas/
cxxv https://pixabay.com/en/china-temple-wheel-of-life-222325/, free for commercial use
cxxvi Cavendish, Richard; Ling, Trevor Oswald (1980), Mythology: an Illustrated Encyclopedia, Rizzoli, pp. 40–45
cxxvii http://www.bbc.co.uk/religion/religions/zoroastrian/beliefs/god.shtml
cxxviii Cavendish, Richard; Ling, Trevor Oswald (1980), Mythology: an Illustrated Encyclopedia, Rizzoli, pp. 40–45
cxxix Abdu'l-Bahá (1982). Some answered questions. Translated by Laura Clifford. Wilmette, Ill.: Bahá'í Publ. Trust.
cxxx https://www.dailyo.in/variety/hindusim-world-creation-universe-brahma-vishu-shiva/story/1/19522.html
cxxxi https://www.britannica.com/topic/purusha-Indian-philosophy
cxxxii https://vedaravindamu.wordpress.com/2011/10/11/origin-of-the-universe-nasadiya-sukta-of-rig-veda/
cxxxiii https://www.consciouslivingfoundation.org/ebooks/13/CLF-brihadaranyaka_upanishad.pdf
cxxxiv Alain Daniélou (11 February 2003). A Brief History of India. Inner Traditions / Bear & Co.
cxxxv https://www.livescience.com/9761-10-animals-tools.html
cxxxvi https://www.world-of-lucid-dreaming.com/10-animals-with-self-awareness.html
cxxxvii http://www.nbcnews.com/id/20393495/ns/technology_and_science-science/t/how-life-earth-began/#.WkkIYSOZPBI
cxxxviii Undeniable: Evolution and the Science of Creation by Bill Nye (Author), St. Martin's Griffin (2015), Edition
cxxxix https://www.answers.com/Q/What_is_the_purpose_of_life_in_Judaism
cxl http://www.thechristiannetwork.com/the-purpose-of-the-christian-life/
cxli https://u.osu.edu/group5/2014/10/12/the-meaning-of-life-according-to-hinduism/comment-page-1/
cxlii https://www.britannica.com/topic/dharma-religious-concept
cxliii https://vedicastrologicalremedies.wordpress.com/2017/02/07/five-rin-debts-of-a-human-being/
cxliv https://www.britannica.com/topic/artha
cxlv https://study.com/academy/lesson/the-four-goals-of-hindu-life-kama-artha-dharma-moksha.html
cxlvi http://www.bbc.co.uk/religion/religions/hinduism/beliefs/moksha.shtml
cxlvii http://www.religionfacts.com/buddhism/meaning-life
cxlviii https://www.lionsroar.com/what-are-the-four-noble-truths/
cxlix https://www.buddha101.com/p_path.htm
cl https://www.islamtomorrow.com/purpose.htm
cli https://www.islam-guide.com/purpose-of-life.htm#s8
clii https://chloemilston.wordpress.com/2013/08/03/society-and-meaningpurpose-of-life/
cliii https://theancientshinto.weebly.com/human-meaning.html
cliv https://www.wicca-spirituality.com/wiccan-belief.html
clv https://commons.wikimedia.org/wiki/File:Red_Giant_Earth_warm.jpg, public domain
clvi http://themoderncatholic.com/catholic-vs-protestant-whats-the-difference/

clvii Heaven: Our Enduring Fascination with the Afterlife by Lisa Miller (Author)Harper Perennial (2011), Edition: Harper Perennial ed., 368 pages
clviii https://www.al-islam.org/man-and-his-destiny-ayatullah-murtadha-mutahhari/part-1-fate-and-destiny-are-words-cause-alarm
clix http://www.answering-islam.org/Quran/Contra/predestination.html
clx http://www.hinduwebsite.com/hinduism/h_death.asp
clxi https://www.dailyo.in/variety/death-moksha-rebirth-punarjanma-hinduism/story/1/17013.html
clxii https://www.near-death.com/reincarnation/research/ian-stevenson.html
clxiii http://www.sptimmortalityproject.com/background/buddhist-views-of-the-afterlife/
clxiv https://www.urbandharma.org/udharma5/viewdeath.html
clxv https://www.rd.com/culture/animals-that-live-forever/
clxvi https://www.ncbi.nlm.nih.gov/pmc/articles/PMC4133289/
clxvii https://commons.wikimedia.org/wiki/File:Turritopsis_dohrnii_(cropped).jpg, public domain
clxviii http://www.physlink.com/education/askexperts/ae261.cfm
clxix https://commons.wikimedia.org/wiki/File:Complete-circle-foodchain.jpg, public domain
clxx https://do-animals-have-souls.info/organised-religions.html
clxxi https://www.logicallyfallacious.com/tools/lp/Bo/LogicalFallacies/145/Proving-Non-Existence
clxxii http://science.howstuffworks.com/science-vs-myth/afterlife/during-near-death-experience.htm
clxxiii https://lnco.epfl.ch/files/content/sites/lnco/files/shared/publications/lnco/2009_Dieguez_NC(chap)_leaving%20body%20and%20life%20behind-out%20of%20body%20and%20near%20death%20experience.pdf
clxxiv Blanke, Olaf (2009). The Neurology of Consciousness. London: London: Academic Publishers, 2009. pp. 303–324.

Chapter 3 Purpose of Religions

clxxv http://www.patheos.com/blogs/daylightatheism/essays/nothing-fails-like-prayer/
clxxvi https://en.wikipedia.org/wiki/Inuit_religion
clxxvii Accession: see Piedras Negras stela 11; illness and burial: Las Casas, in Miles 1957: 750, 773; drought: Landa, in Tozzer 1941: 54, 180–181
clxxviii http://mayansandtikal.com/mayan-civilisation/mayan-sacrifice/, public domain
clxxix https://www.scientificamerican.com/article/1959-cargo-cults-melanesia/
clxxx https://commons.wikimedia.org/wiki/File:JohnFrumCrossTanna1967.jpg, public domain
clxxxi https://www.express.co.uk/news/science/848991/life-after-death-what-happens-when-you-die-quantum-physics
clxxxii http://www.patheos.com/blogs/daylightatheism/essays/nothing-fails-like-prayer/
clxxxiii http://www.patheos.com/blogs/friendlyatheist/2013/11/28/are-religious-people-really-more-generous-than-atheists-a-new-study-puts-that-myth-to-rest/
clxxxiv http://www.politicalsystems.com/theocracy.html
clxxxv https://en.wikipedia.org/wiki/Ali_Khamenei#/media/File:Ali_Khamenei_crop.jpg,

public domain
[clxxxvi] https://en.wikipedia.org/wiki/File:Martin_Luther,_1529.jpg, public domain
[clxxxvii] https://oi.uchicago.edu/research/symposia/religion-and-power-divine-kingship-ancient-world-and-beyond-0
[clxxxviii] http://wwww.emmitsburg.net/archive_list/articles/thoughtful/amir/religion_in_middle_east.htm
[clxxxix] http://www.rodneyohebsion.com/religion-uses.htm
[cxc] https://en.wikipedia.org/wiki/List_of_religious_leaders_convicted_of_crimes
[cxci] https://arcjohn.wordpress.com/social-control-religion/
[cxcii] http://glenscorgie.com/2012/10/07/pulpits-and-politics-dont-mix/
[cxciii] https://commons.wikimedia.org/wiki/File:Jerry_Falwell_portrait.jpg, public domain
[cxciv] http://www.pewresearch.org/fact-tank/2014/07/22/in-30-countries-heads-of-state-must-belong-to-a-certain-religion/
[cxcv] https://www.ncbi.nlm.nih.gov/pmc/articles/PMC4345965/
[cxcvi] https://www.stevepavlina.com/blog/2008/05/10-reasons-you-should-never-have-a-religion/
[cxcvii] http://www.queen.clara.net/10.html
[cxcviii] https://en.wikipedia.org/wiki/Church_tax
[cxcix] http://www.pressherald.com/2016/09/16/religion-is-big-business-study-shows/
[cc] Inside Scientology: The Story of America's Most Secretive Religion by Janet Reitman, Mariner Books (2013)
[cci] https://en.wikipedia.org/wiki/L._Ron_Hubbard
[ccii] https://commons.wikimedia.org/wiki/File:L._Ron_Hubbard_in_1950.jpg, public domain
[cciii] http://www.beliefnet.com/faiths/christianity/8-richest-pastors-in-america.aspx?p=6
[cciv] https://en.wikipedia.org/wiki/Jim_Bakker
[ccv] https://www.flickr.com/photos/28698046@N08/22407116907, public domain
[ccvi] https://en.wikipedia.org/wiki/Oral_Roberts
[ccvii] http://califias.blogspot.com/2015/01/wesley-swift-and-church-of-jesus-christ.html
[ccviii] https://www.christianitytoday.com/history/issues/issue-33/why-christians-supported-slavery.html
[ccix] McKim, Donald K. (2011). More Presbyterian Questions, More Presbyterian Answers: Exploring Christian Faith. Westminster John Knox Press. p. 72.
[ccx] http://atheistfoundation.org.au/article/overcoming-religious-indoctrination-6-steps-towards-sanity/

Chapter 4 Validity of Religions

[ccxi]
http://www.qcc.cuny.edu/socialsciences/ppecorino/phil_of_religion_text/CHAPTER_5_ARGUMENTS_EXPERIENCE/Burden-of-Proof.htm
[ccxii] https://www.merriam-webster.com/dictionary/fact
[ccxiii] https://dictionary.law.com/Default.aspx?selected=1586
[ccxiv] http://www.jewfaq.org/beliefs.htm
[ccxv] https://www.blueletterbible.org/faq/don_stewart/don_stewart_1301.cfm
[ccxvi] https://www.allaboutphilosophy.org/proof-that-god-exists-faq.htm

ccxvii https://www.space.com/21800-alien-planets-60-billion-habitable-exoplanets.html
ccxviii https://science.howstuffworks.com/planets--universe-support-life.htm
ccxix Burchell, M.J. (2006). "W(h)ither the Drake equation?". International Journal of Astrobiology. 5 (3): 243–250.
ccxx Forgan, D. (2009). "A numerical testbed for hypotheses of extraterrestrial life and intelligence". International Journal of Astrobiology. 8 (2)
ccxxi https://infidels.org/library/modern/donald_morgan/contradictions.html
ccxxii http://www.beholdthebeast.com/contradictions_in_the_koran.htm
ccxxiii https://www.livescience.com/8008-bible-possibly-written-centuries-earlier-text-suggests.html
ccxxiv http://www.bc.edu/schools/stm/crossroads/resources/birthofjesus/intro/the_dating_of_thegospels.html
ccxxv Chronology of Prophetic Events, Fazlur Rehman Shaikh (2001) p. 50 Ta-Ha Publishers Ltd.
ccxxvi http://biblehub.com/numbers/16-32.htm
ccxxvii https://www.biblegateway.com/passage/?search=Luke+16&version=NIV
ccxxviii https://theheartopener.wordpress.com/lets-ponder/description-of-hell-in-islam/
ccxxix https://www.universetoday.com/65661/what-is-the-center-of-the-earth-made-of/
ccxxx http://www.bbc.com/earth/story/20150814-what-is-at-the-centre-of-the-earth
ccxxxi https://commons.wikimedia.org/wiki/File:Earth_poster.svg, public domain
ccxxxii http://www.islamcan.com/hell-jahannam/the-fuel-of-hell-fire.shtml
ccxxxiii http://www.cracked.com/blog/4-people-who-died-went-to-hell-then-came-back/
ccxxxiv Joseph Hell Die Religion des Islam Motilal Banarsidass Publishe 1915
ccxxxv https://kaddish-prayer.com/wiki/kaddish
ccxxxvi http://www.askmoses.com/en/article/287,2164280/What-is-the-purpose-of-reciting-Kaddish-for-a-departed-family-member.html
ccxxxvii https://biblia.com/bible/esv/Acts%201.9–11
ccxxxviii http://ebenalexander.com/books/proof-of-heaven/
ccxxxix http://www.dummies.com/religion/hinduism/core-beliefs-of-hindus/
ccxl http://www.pbs.org/edens/thailand/buddhism.htm
ccxli https://www.jainworld.com/jainbooks/antiquity/doctjain.htm
ccxlii https://www.britannica.com/topic/Jainism
ccxliii http://www.bbc.co.uk/religion/religions/jainism/beliefs/threejewels.shtml
ccxliv http://www.bbc.co.uk/religion/religions/sikhism/beliefs/beliefs.shtml
ccxlv http://www.sikhismguide.org/sikh-belief.php
ccxlvi http://www.sikhismguide.org/sikh-belief.php
ccxlvii http://www.sikhismguide.org/sikh-belief.php
ccxlviii https://www.npr.org/2014/01/05/259886077/searching-for-science-behind-reincarnation
ccxlix https://www.express.co.uk/news/science/716499/reincarnation-REAL-proof-life-after-death
ccl https://www.psychologytoday.com/us/blog/biocentrism/201112/does-the-soul-exist-evidence-says-yes
ccli Stiff: The Curious Lives of Human Cadavers by Mary Roach
cclii https://www.polytheism.net
ccliii https://www.ancient.eu/Greek_Religion/

ccliv https://www.metmuseum.org/toah/hd/dbag/hd_dbag.htm
cclv https://www.allabouthistory.org/ancient-romans-faq.htm
cclvi http://myweb.usf.edu/~liottan/theegyptiansoul.html
cclvii https://www.ancient.eu/Egyptian_Book_of_the_Dead/
cclviii https://en.wikipedia.org/wiki/Maat#/media/File:BD_Weighing_of_the_Heart.jpg, pubic domain
cclix https://www.thoughtco.com/too-many-gods-too-many-religions-248240
cclx http://theconversation.com/is-religion-a-force-for-good-35061
cclxi http://www.pewresearch.org/fact-tank/2016/08/24/why-americas-nones-left-religion-behind/
cclxii https://en.m.wikipedia.org/wiki/File:Religions_of_the_United_States.png, public domain
cclxiii https://www.huffingtonpost.com/phil-zuckerman/religion-declining-secula_b_9889398.html
cclxiv https://www.thetimes.co.uk/article/post-christian-britain-arrives-as-majority-say-they-have-no-religion-5bzxzdcl6p3

Part 2 Implications of Religion

cclxv http://www.debate.org/opinions/is-religion-good-for-the-world

Chapter 1 Community

cclxvi https://en.wikipedia.org/wiki/Sigmund_Freud%27s_views_on_religion
cclxvii
https://commons.wikimedia.org/wiki/File:Alauddin%27s_Madrasa,_Qutb_complex.jpg , public domain
cclxviii http://christianaggression.org/2016/04/28/conversion-tactics-charitable-allurement/
cclxix http://www.pewforum.org/2003/06/04/ministering-to-those-in-need-the-rights-and-wrongs-of-missions-and-humanitarian-assistance-in-iraq/
cclxx https://www.ncbi.nlm.nih.gov/pmc/articles/PMC2598091/
cclxxi https://quizlet.com/186044689/buddhism-study-guide-flash-cards/
cclxxii
https://books.google.com/books?id=3MK5u1_7CLYC&pg=PA300&lpg=PA300&dq=dharma+bhanaks&source=bl&ots=-PkI4MIOJU&sig=UxajWphPEYHMnuZVggJl2SL-gwg&hl=en&sa=X&ved=0ahUKEwiuypCxuMzaAhVCNd8KHbgiC3kQ6AEINDAC#v=onepage&q=dharma%20bhanaks&f=false
cclxxiii http://www.qosqo.com/catedral.shtml
cclxxiv http://www.beliefnet.com/faiths/christianity/galleries/7-reasons-christians-dont-share-their-faith.aspx?p=9
cclxxv http://www.patheos.com/blogs/godlessindixie/2017/06/14/christians-dont-like-sharing-faith/
cclxxvi http://www.akha.org/content/commentary/theblackhand.html
cclxxvii https://en.wikipedia.org/wiki/Faith-based_foreign_aid
cclxxviii https://en.wikipedia.org/wiki/List_of_religions_and_spiritual_traditions

201

Chapter 2 Acceptable and Unacceptable Behaviors

[cclxxix] http://bn2buddhism.blogspot.com/2009/10/what-do-buddhist-wear.html
[cclxxx] Sex and the Constitution: Sex, Religion, and Law from America's Origins to the Twenty-First Century by Geoffrey R. Stone, Liveright (2017)
[cclxxxi] https://en.wikipedia.org/wiki/Sharia
[cclxxxii] https://en.wikipedia.org/wiki/Sharia#/media/File:Apostasy_laws_in_2013.SVG, public domain
[cclxxxiii] https://www.buddhanet.net/e-learning/budethics.htm
[cclxxxiv] https://ipfs.io/ipfs/QmXoypizjW3WknFiJnKLwHCnL72vedxjQkDDP1mXWo6uco/wiki/Brahmajala_Sutra_(Mahayana).html
[cclxxxv] https://www.buddhanet.net/e-learning/budethics.htm
[cclxxxvi] https://ipfs.io/ipfs/QmXoypizjW3WknFiJnKLwHCnL72vedxjQkDDP1mXWo6uco/wiki/Brahmajala_Sutra_(Mahayana).html
[cclxxxvii] https://en.wikipedia.org/wiki/Sin
[cclxxxviii] http://www.hinduism.co.za/ethics.htm
[cclxxxix] http://www.bbc.co.uk/religion/religions/hinduism/hinduethics/animal.shtml
[ccxc] https://islamqa.info/en/200632
[ccxci] http://www.jewishvirtuallibrary.org/the-seven-noachide-laws
[ccxcii] http://www.jewfaq.org/613.htm
[ccxciii] https://www.indy100.com/article/polygamy-around-the-world-map-reddit-7621171
[ccxciv] https://en.wikipedia.org/wiki/File:Polygamy_World_Map.png, public domain
[ccxcv] https://en.wikipedia.org/wiki/Oneida_Community
[ccxcvi] https://commons.wikimedia.org/wiki/File:John_Humphrey_Noyes.jpg, public domain
[ccxcvii] https://en.wikipedia.org/wiki/Shakers
[ccxcviii] https://commons.wikimedia.org/wiki/File:Life_of_the_Diligent_Shaker.jpg, public domain
[ccxcix] Sex and the Constitution: Sex, Religion, and Law from America's Origins to the Twenty-First Century by Geoffrey R. Stone (Author), Liveright (2017)
[ccc] https://www.biblegateway.com/passage/?search=Leviticus+20%3A13
[ccci] https://en.wikipedia.org/wiki/Homosexuality_and_religion
[cccii] https://en.wikipedia.org/wiki/Sharia
[ccciii] https://kinseyconfidential.org/kinsey-10-percent-homosexuality-myth/
[ccciv] http://news.gallup.com/poll/6961/what-percentage-population-gay.aspx
[cccv] https://en.wikipedia.org/wiki/Religious_views_on_masturbation
[cccvi] Wile (1994), p. 59.
[cccvii] https://en.wikipedia.org/wiki/Religion_and_abortion
[cccviii] Bahá'u'lláh; Abdu'l-Bahá; Shoghi Effendi; Universal House of Justice (1983). Hornby, Helen, ed. Lights of Guidance: A Bahá'í Reference File. New Delhi: Bahá'í Publishing Trust.
[cccix] http://www.bbc.co.uk/religion/religions/rastafari/ataglance/glance.shtml
[cccx] https://en.wikipedia.org/wiki/Digambara
[cccxi] https://en.wikipedia.org/wiki/Sadhu
[cccxii] https://en.wikipedia.org/wiki/Skyclad_(Neopaganism)

cccxiii https://commons.wikimedia.org/wiki/File:Acharya5.jpg, public domain
cccxiv https://en.wikipedia.org/wiki/Religious_clothing
cccxv https://sco.m.wikipedia.org/wiki/File:Burqa_IMG_1127.jpg, public domain
cccxvi
https://commons.wikimedia.org/wiki/File:Aron_Marcus_(1800)_1880_by_Ernst_Joseph son.jpg, public domain
cccxvii http://www.bbc.co.uk/religion/religions/sikhism/ritesrituals/amrit.shtml
cccxviii http://www.bbc.co.uk/religion/religions/sikhism/customs/fiveks.shtml
cccxix https://commons.wikimedia.org/wiki/File:Kirpan_with_ruler.jpg, public domain
cccxx http://www.bbc.co.uk/religion/religions/rastafari/ataglance/glance.shtml
cccxxi https://www.myjewishlearning.com/article/three-blessings/
cccxxii https://torah.org/learning/women-class31/
cccxxiii https://en.wikipedia.org/wiki/Gender_and_religion
cccxxiv https://commons.wikimedia.org/wiki/File:Sati_ceremony.jpg, public domain
cccxxv
https://commons.wikimedia.org/wiki/File:Slaves_Zadib_Yemen_13th_century_BNF_Paris.jpg, public domain
cccxxvi
http://www.cnn.com/interactive/2012/03/world/mauritania.slaverys.last.stronghold/index.html
cccxxvii
https://commons.wikimedia.org/wiki/File:Invitation_to_Sanpete_by_Jerry_Anderson.jpg, public domain
cccxxviii http://www.bbc.com/news/uk-27324224
cccxxix http://www.bbc.co.uk/religion/religions/jainism/ataglance/glance.shtml
cccxxx https://www.deseretnews.com/top/714/5/Mormonism-Dietary-guidelines-of-some-of-the-worlds-major-religions.html
cccxxxi https://en.wikipedia.org/wiki/Ital
cccxxxii https://spirituality.knoji.com/ritual-cannibalism-past-and-present/
cccxxxiii https://www.flickr.com/photos/naishh/32404971674, public domain
cccxxxiv https://www.historyofvaccines.org/content/articles/cultural-perspectives-vaccination
cccxxxv http://listverse.com/2008/01/28/top-10-evils-of-scientology/
cccxxxvi https://commons.wikimedia.org/wiki/File:Scientology_psychiatry_kills.jpg, public domain
cccxxxvii http://shintoismproject.weebly.com/shinto-ethics.html

Chapter 3 Positive Aspects of Religion

cccxxxviii https://www.merriam-webster.com/dictionary/moral
cccxxxix https://en.wikipedia.org/wiki/Sigmund_Freud%27s_views_on_religion
cccxl https://www.sharefaith.com/blog/2013/06/top-4-christian-humanitarian-organizations-fighting-poverty-slavery-world-hunger/
cccxli https://www.theregister.co.uk/2008/11/30/tzu_chi_foundation/
cccxlii https://www.sewausa.org
cccxliii https://www.amnesty.org.uk
cccxliv https://www.unicef.org.uk

203

cccxlv
https://donate.doctorswithoutborders.org/onetime.cfm?source=ADD180U0U01&utm_source=AdWords&utm_medium=ppc&utm_campaign=GooglePaid&utm_content=branded&gclid=EAIaIQobChMI8Ibsruvi2QIVBlYNCh1VQgIAEAAYASAAEgKRz_D_BwE

cccxlvi https://www.wateraid.org/us/

cccxlvii http://news.berkeley.edu/2012/04/30/religionandgenerosity/

Chapter 4 Persecution

cccxlviii http://www.pewresearch.org/fact-tank/2017/06/09/christians-faced-widespread-harassment-in-2015-but-mostly-in-christian-majority-countries/ft_17-06-09_christianpersecution/

cccxlix https://en.wikipedia.org/wiki/Religious_persecution

cccl https://www.sikhnet.com/news/islamic-india-biggest-holocaust-world-history

cccli https://www.sikhnet.com/news/islamic-india-biggest-holocaust-world-history

ccclii https://www.britannica.com/topic/Islamic-caste

cccliii
http://www.chinabuddhismencyclopedia.com/en/index.php?title=Persecution_of_Buddhists

cccliv http://www.ancient-origins.net/history/manichaeism-one-most-popular-religions-ancient-world-002658

ccclv http://education.asianart.org/explore-resources/background-information/buddhism-tang-618–906-and-song-960–1279-dynasties

ccclvi https://www.zum.de/whkmla/sp/1112/sbk/sbk2.html

ccclvii https://en.wikipedia.org/wiki/Anti-Jewish_pogroms_in_the_Russian_Empire

ccclviii https://en.wikipedia.org/wiki/The_Holocaust#/media/File:Stroop_Report_-_Warsaw_Ghetto_Uprising_06b.jpg, public domain

ccclix
https://www.google.com/search?as_st=y&tbm=isch&hl=en&as_q=stoning+of+stephen&as_epq=&as_oq=&as_eq=&cr=&as_sitesearch=&safe=images&tbs=sur:fc#imgrc=upjSIdEOIteaYM:, public domain

ccclx https://en.wikipedia.org/wiki/Buddhism_and_violence

ccclxi https://www.americamagazine.org/faith/2018/01/11/top-10-worst-countries-christian-persecution

ccclxii https://en.wikipedia.org/wiki/Joseph_Smith

ccclxiii https://en.wikipedia.org/wiki/Anti-Mormonism#/media/File:G._W._Fasel_-_Charles_G._Crehen_-_Nagel_%26_Weingaertner_-_Martyrdom_of_Joseph_and_Hiram_Smith_in_Carthage_jail,_June_27th,_1844.jpg, public domain

ccclxiv The Modern Scholar: Heaven or Heresy: A History of the Inquisition by Thomas F. Madden, Recorded Books (Publisher), Recorded Books (2008)

ccclxv http://www.cathar.info/cathar_beliefs.htm

ccclxvi https://www.britannica.com/topic/Waldenses

ccclxvii https://en.wikipedia.org/wiki/Spanish_Inquisition#/media/File:An_auto-da-fé_of_the_Spanish_Inquisition_and_the_execution_o_Wellcome_V0041892.jpg, public domain

ccclxviii https://www.livescience.com/55431-infamous-witch-trials-in-history.html

ccclxix http://gregladen.com/blog/2017/10/08/how-many-people-were-killed-as-witches-in-europe-from-1200-to-the-present/
ccclxx http://cphpost.dk/history/denmarks-answer-to-salem-took-place-in-ribe-and-involved-a-king.html
ccclxxi https://www.history.com/topics/salem-witch-trials
ccclxxii https://commons.wikimedia.org/wiki/File:Witchcraft_at_Salem_Village.jpg, public domain
ccclxxiii https://www.britannica.com/biography/Sant-Jarnail-Singh-Bhindranwale
ccclxxiv https://en.wikipedia.org/wiki/Golden_Temple#/media/File:Hamandir_Sahib_(Golden_Temple).jpg, public domain
ccclxxv https://en.wikipedia.org/wiki/Islamic_State_of_Iraq_and_the_Levant

Chapter 5 Religious Wars

ccclxxvi https://www.counterextremism.com/content/isiss-persecution-religions
ccclxxvii https://constantlyreforming.wordpress.com/every-battle-in-the-bible/
ccclxxviii https://www.chabad.org/library/article_cdo/aid/1942076/jewish/Biblical-Guidelines-for-Warfare.htm
ccclxxix "Zionism" Oxford Dictionary
ccclxxx https://www.britannica.com/event/Battle-of-Badr
ccclxxxi http://corpus.quran.com/translation.jsp?chapter=3&verse=123
ccclxxxii Answering Jihad: A Better Way Forward by Nabeel Qureshi, Zondervan (2016)
ccclxxxiii https://commons.wikimedia.org/wiki/File:Battle_of_Badr.jpg, public domain
ccclxxxiv https://www.independent.co.uk/news/world/middle-east/sunni-and-shia-islams-1400-year-old-divide-explained-a6796131.html
ccclxxxv https://theconversation.com/what-is-the-shia-sunni-divide-78216
ccclxxxvi https://en.wikipedia.org/wiki/Abdul-Aziz_bin_Muhammad
ccclxxxvii https://www.e-ir.info/2016/02/07/the-iran-iraq-war-the-use-of-religion-as-a-tool/
ccclxxxviii https://www.dw.com/en/sunnis-shiites-locked-in-an-endless-conflict/a-18958491
ccclxxxix http://www.indiastudychannel.com/resources/146940-Sir-Jadunath-Sarkar-Life-and-Education-biography.aspx
cccxc https://commons.wikimedia.org/wiki/File:Sultan-Mahmud-Ghaznawi.jpg, public domain
cccxci God Wills It!: Understanding the Crusades, Professor Thomas Madden, The Modern Scholar
cccxcii https://commons.wikimedia.org/wiki/File:Holy_Family_Catholic_Church_(Oldenburg,_Indiana)_-_stained_glass,_Melchizedek_window_detail,_knight.jpg, public domain
cccxciii https://en.wikipedia.org/wiki/Crusader_states
cccxciv https://en.wikipedia.org/wiki/Islam_and_war
cccxcv https://commons.wikimedia.org/wiki/File:Map_Crusader_states_1165-en.svg, public domain
cccxcvi http://lostislamichistory.com/the-crusades-part-3-liberation/
cccxcvii http://www.historyofwar.org/articles/battles_hattin.html
cccxcviii Richard P. Bonney, Jihad: From Qu'ran to Bin Laden; Palgrave Macmillan:

Hampshire, 2004
cccxcix

[cccxcix] https://commons.wikimedia.org/wiki/File:Suleiman_the_Magnificent_of_the_Ottoman_Empire.jpg, public domain
[cd] http://www.sanghol.edu.in/shri/babar_1.php
[cdi] http://www.historydiscussion.net/history-of-india/battle-of-khanwa-causes-events-and-consequences/2764
[cdii] https://aeon.co/essays/the-great-aurangzeb-is-everybodys-least-favourite-mughal
[cdiii] https://www.britannica.com/biography/Aurangzeb
[cdiv] https://www.sscnet.ucla.edu/southasia/History/Mughals/Aurang.html
[cdv] https://en.wikipedia.org/wiki/Religious_war
[cdvi] https://en.wikipedia.org/wiki/Adal_Sultanate
[cdvii] https://www.wardheernews.com/defending-somalia-then-and-now/, permission granted 23 September 2018
[cdviii] Chronik des Johannes Stumpf, 1548. Scanned from Schwabe & Co.: Geschichte der Schweiz und der Schweizer, Schwabe & Co 1986/2004. ISBN 3-796-52067-7.
[cdix] https://whistlinginthewind.org/2012/05/23/religion-as-a-cause-of-war-in-ireland/
[cdx] https://en.wikipedia.org/wiki/Irish_Rebellion_of_1641
[cdxi] https://en.wikipedia.org/wiki/Oliver_Cromwell
[cdxii] https://en.wikipedia.org/wiki/Williamite_War_in_Ireland
[cdxiii] https://en.wikipedia.org/wiki/Irish_Rebellion_of_1798
cdxiv
https://www.google.com/search?as_st=y&tbm=isch&hl=en&as_q=irish+rebellion+of+1798&as_epq=&as_oq=&as_eq=&cr=&as_sitesearch=&safe=images&tbs=sur:fc#imgrc=YdSQi4Mkl2PkGM:, public domain
[cdxv] https://en.wikipedia.org/wiki/French_Wars_of_Religion#cite_note-1
[cdxvi] La masacre de San Bartolomé, por François Dubois.jpg, public domain
[cdxvii] Peter Snayers - Spanischer Überfall auf ein flämisches Dorf.jpg
[cdxviii] https://www.historyguy.com/Barbary_Wars.html#.Wt4iQy-ZMxg
[cdxix] https://www.truthorfiction.com/jefferson-vs-muslims/
[cdxx] http://eng.islam-today.ru/history/the-role-of-sheikh-ul-islam-in-the-ottoman-empire/
[cdxxi] https://www.history.com/this-day-in-history/ottoman-empire-declares-a-holy-war
[cdxxii] https://en.wikipedia.org/wiki/Religious_violence_in_India
[cdxxiii] https://en.wikipedia.org/wiki/Religious_war
[cdxxiv] https://en.wikipedia.org/wiki/Indo-Pakistani_wars_and_conflicts
[cdxxv] Partition_of_India.PNG, public domain
[cdxxvi] https://en.wikipedia.org/wiki/Ngo_Dinh_Diem, public domain
[cdxxvii] https://www.blackpast.org/global-african-history/events-global-african-history/first-sudanese-civil-war-1955-1972/
[cdxxviii] https://www.encyclopedia.com/social-sciences-and-law/sociology-and-social-reform/sociology-general-terms-and-concepts/lebanese
[cdxxix] https://en.wikipedia.org/wiki/Second_Sudanese_Civil_War
[cdxxx] https://en.wikipedia.org/wiki/Yugoslav_Wars
[cdxxxi] https://en.wikipedia.org/wiki/Yugoslav_Wars
cdxxxii
https://ca.wikipedia.org/wiki/Boko_Haram#/media/File:Milice_d%27autodéfense_Nigeria_2015.JPG, public domain

cdxxxiii https://en.wikipedia.org/wiki/Boko_Haram_insurgency
cdxxxiv https://www.wired.com/2001/09/osama-in-e-mail/
cdxxxv https://www.theguardian.com/world/2002/nov/24/theobserver
cdxxxvi https://www.biblegateway.com/passage/?search=1+Timothy+6%3A10&version=NIV
cdxxxvii https://www.scientificamerican.com/article/how-to-convince-someone-when-facts-fail/
cdxxxviii https://www.newyorker.com/magazine/2017/02/27/why-facts-dont-change-our-minds

www.ingramcontent.com/pod-product-compliance
Lightning Source LLC
LaVergne TN
LVHW041617070426
835507LV00008B/295